DALÍ

A perverse life

OTHER SUCCESSFUL BOOKS BY JOAN CASTELLAR-GASSOL
in this collection

"The personality of Gaudí, narrated in a simple, easy manner. The reader would like the book, instead of having just 140 pages, to have two or three thousand!"

FERRAN RODRIGUEZ, *architect. "Flame", magazine Toronto, Ontario*, Canada

"A splendid book, written in the style of the discerning populariser who knows how to capture the reader from beginning to end."

P. RAIMONDO SORGIA, O.P., *director of "Sammarcoradio", Florence*, Italy

---

Also published in Catalan, Castilian, French, German and Italian

---

"The chronicles included in *BARCELONA: A HISTORY* drink from the sources of the great authors and do not skimp even on minor information, the type which describes everyday life, nor on the recourse to a contemporary style which is proper to journalism, a discipline which the author knows well."

IGNASI ARAGAY, *Avui* newspaper, Barcelona, Catalonia

Also published in Catalan, Castilian and French

"I am impressed by how the author has been able to combine into a unified whole the allegorical and esoteric elements of Montserrat with true, documented history, without affecting the tone and pace of the narration at any moment."

ANTONI DALMAU, *writer, Barcelona*, Catalonia

"This book (which is not a tourist guide) deals with the mountains and the Benedictine monastery of Montserrat from the most mystical-religious aspect to the most touristic facet, by way of geography and history."

"L'enllaç", Igualada, Catalonia

Also published in Catalan, Castilian and French

JOAN CASTELLAR-GASSOL

DALÍ

A perverse life

English translation by Paul Martin

Edicions de 1984
Barcelona

Dalí, una vida perversa
© Joan Castellar-Gassol

First edition: March 2002
Design: Enric Satué
For the illustrations by Salvador Dalí, © Salvador Dalí,
Fundació Gala-Salvador Dalí, VEGAP, 2002
English translation: Paul Martin
© for this edition: Edicions de 1984, s.l.
Pujades, 74-80, 08005 Barcelona
e-mail:1984@edicions1984.com

ISBN: 84-86540-94-1
Legal deposit: B. 10127-2002

Printed in Catalonia
Photocomposition: Víctor Igual, S. L.
Printed by Novagràfik, Pol. Ind. Foinvasa, Vivaldi, 5
08110 Montcada i Reixac

INDEX

"I will be a genius and the world will admire me"

PREFACE

I met Dalí in 1965, when I interviewed him for the Hispano-American magazine *Índice*. I had recently returned home from Paris, where I had published a number of chronicles in *Les Lettres Nouvelles*, the magazine directed by Maurice Nadeau, the leading historian of the Surrealist movement.

By the 1960's, Surrealism as a pictorial movement was dead and buried, but the scandals and stunts Salvador Dalí had staged in both Europe and the USA had brought the Catalan painter controversial worldwide fame which, after his death in 1989, has been further swelled by all kinds of interests and circumstances.

My research in archives and newspaper libraries has provided me with the basic information for briefly reconstructing decisive episodes and situations in the life of the artist who, at the age of 16, wrote, "I will be a genius and the world will admire me"; the artist whom the eminent Catalan journalist Manuel Brunet called "the foremost pornographer of our time."

And finally, if I had to give readers a warning, it could only be this from the classics: *Cave canem*, beware of the dog!

THE AUTHOR

PART ONE

CHAPTER 1

Spring fashion

New York, 16 March 1939

Manhattan was a spectacle.

From the windows of the restaurant on the 65th floor of the Rockefeller Center, you could almost have touched the clouds. Tuxedoed millionaires accompanied by young blondes with their plunging necklines and cigarette-holders gazed down at 5th Avenue and the rest of the city of the seven deadly sins laid out at their feet.

Not everyone in the USA had recovered from the long-lasting consequences of the 1929 Wall Street Crash, and the display windows of the elegant Bonwit-Teller clothes store, standing between the Rockefeller building and East 51st Street, attracted crowds of passers-by who had to be content with just looking.

That evening there were more such onlookers in front of the store than was to be expected in a district like Manhattan, where novelties had become the routine. To present the new line of spring fashion, one of the Bonwit-Teller windows featured a conventionally-dressed dummy. But the next window displayed a pile of weird, disgusting junk. What, for instance, was a bathtub brimming with dirty water doing there?

The onlookers squashing their noses against the glass saw an infuriated man with a black moustache, who looked like a French cook, having a furious row with on of the store assistants. And what was that moustachioed madman

Rockefeller Center, 65th floor, 1939. A watercolour by the Catalan painter Josep Simont.
(AA)

trying to do now, shoving the bathtub towards the window?

The front-row spectators were unable to pull back in
time. The window pane shattered into a thousand sparkling fragments, and the overturned bathtub and the water
and the moustachioed lunatic tumbled out onto the side-
walk at the feet of the terrified passers-by.

The second part of the incident – or performance? –
took place in the district police station situated in East 51st
Street, just a few paces away from the store.

The character with the moustache who had caused the
havoc was Caucasian – as the American police called whites –

5'7", age 34; his passport said he was an artist and that he was a native of Figueres, Spain. Name of the detained: Salvador Dalí.

Judge Louis B. Brodsky, in charge of the case, who was well aware that the law was made for all but that not all were equal before that law, was informed that the detained individual had irreproachable contacts in the city – people related with the mighty Morgan Bank – and that three years earlier *Time* magazine had dedicated its illustrious cover to the accused. Being who he was, therefore, Dalí was merely ordered to pay for the window he had broken.

The following day, the artist gladly declared to the city's scandal-hungry newshounds that he had lost his temper with the staff of Bonwit-Teller because the store had commissioned him to decorate the display window but at the last moment had not respected the artist's freedom; they had changed the Surrealist dummy that he had installed there for an orthodox one.

Among other details, Dalí had imagined the bathtub as a pond in a macabre stage set. Three horrible wax hands belonging to invisible drowned bodies emerged from the surface of the murky water. At the side, lying on a bed, a dove coughed up blood. The dummy was a skeleton covered with spider's webs.

The disconcerting new spring fashions were presented in a manner slightly too horrific even for the dubious tastes of the snobbish owners of Bonwit-Teller and their potential customers, who had long since passed the age of innocence.

Dalí, knowing full well that the scandal would make his stock soar, told the reporters that one of his favourite mottos was, "Let them talk about me all they want, even if it's good!" And sure enough, the event filled column after column in the New York papers, which of course fitted in with the artist's plans perfectly. Just five days before the bathtub incident, the art gallery owned by the wealthy Jewish dealer Julien Levy had had the pleasure of inviting

15

its select clientele to the opening of an exhibition of paintings and objects by Dalí. The titles Dalí had conjured up for the three major paintings were aptly suited to the obscure tastes of Levy's clients: *The Great One-Eyed Cretin, The Sacred Siphon* and *The Imperial Violets*.

The exhibition was a great commercial success, so much so that the emblematic *Life* magazine dedicated to the artist the greatest praise one could hope to hear in the Babel-like city that had replaced the God of the founding fathers of the American nation with the idol of the dollar: "Dalí is one of the richest young artists in the world."

The world might be bursting into flames – the last embers of the civil war in Dalí's home country were still smouldering as the Nazi troops occupied Czechoslovakia and set off shock waves throughout Europe and America – yes, the world might be bursting into flames, but what mattered in 5th Avenue was the dollar.

The artist announced that he worked on the basis of the 'paranoico-critical method.' The confession of a madman, or a joke worthy of the Marx Brothers?

CHAPTER 2

The edge of the precipice

Salvador Dalí Domènech was born on 11 May 1904 in Figueres, a pleasant town which then had some 11,000 inhabitants, situated in the Empordà region of Catalonia, in the north-east corner of the Iberian Peninsula, just a few kilometres from the Costa Brava and the Mediterranean.

Figueres has formed part of the Spanish-governed part of Catalonia since the occupation of 1714, but the nearest big city is Perpinyà (Perpignan) over the border in northern Catalonia, which has been under French administration since the mid-17th century. The border dividing the Spanish and French states lies only thirty kilometres from Figueres, and this proximity to France has always had a powerful influence on the Empordà and the rest of Catalonia.

The Dalí family had enjoyed a comfortable home for two generations. The future Surrealist artist found it natural to have been born in a bed of roses and brought up by a nursemaid. But like the great majority of Catalan families, all of young Salvador's distant forebears on both sides had eked out a living bent double in the fields or ruining their hands and eyesight with tradesmen's tools.

The first documented Dalí ancestor is one Pere, registered in 1568 in the village of Llers, situated a few kilometres north-west of Figueres and inhabited at the time by some seventy families. Pere Dalí was a blacksmith, and the

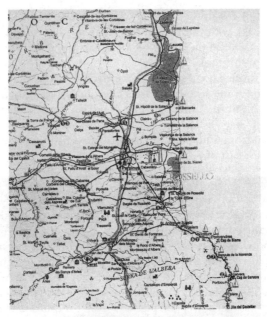

Partial map of the north-eastern end of the Catalan countries. The broken line indicates the Spanish-French state frontier. To the north, the Rosselló (French-governed Catalonia); to the south, the Empordà region of Spanish-governed Catalonia. (AA)

View of Figueres (GdC)

18

façade of his house, now known as Can Fortiana, is still conserved, with the keystone bearing its date of construction or renovation, 1560, beside a carving representing a blacksmith's tools.

In those days, trades were handed down from father to son, and some seven centuries later, in Napoleonic times, the blacksmith of Llers, named Pere Dalí Ragué, a descendant of that earlier Pere, is recorded to have married a woman from Cadaqués, then an isolated fishing village on the coast east of Figueres.

Upper part of the arched doorway of the smithy occupied in 1715 by Gregori Dalí, a direct ancestor of the artist, in the village of Llers. (AL)

It was in Cadaqués that the artist's paternal great-grandfather and grandfather were born, as was his father. The great-grandfather, Salvador Dalí Cucanyes, married a woman from the nearby fishing town of Roses. The grandfather, Gal Dalí Vinyes, in turn married a widow, Teresa Cusí, also from Roses, who had a son by her first marriage.

In the year 1900, the father, Salvador Dalí Cusí, a notary by profession, married Felipa Domènech Ferrés, daughter

19

of a landowning family of Barcelona; the wedding ceremony was held in the Catalan capital itself. The 26-year-old bride was cheerful and good-looking if slightly plump, with black hair and shiny dark eyes. If her husband's looks denoted the rugged features of rural folk, hers revealed a certain urban distinction. He was the forceful, extravert male; she was the discreet female who kept her troubles to herself.

After the wedding, the couple went to live in a spacious rented flat in Figueres, where Salvador had his office.

The artist's parents:
Felipa Domènech Ferrés and Salvador Dalí Cusí. (FD)

The Catalan surname Dalí – emphasis on "lí" – comes from the old German *Adalin*, deriving from *adel* meaning 'noble'. This etymology is explained by the fact that the first County of Barcelona, which virtually constituted early Catalonia itself, came into being as a dependency of the kingdom of the Franks, a people of Germanic origin. It was the Franks, led by a son of the Emperor Charlemagne, who liberated Barcelona from Muslim rule in the year 801. As a result, many Germanic names were introduced into Catalonia and borne not only by the ethnic Franks themselves but also by native Catalans of Gallo-Roman or Hispano-Roman descent.

The Dalí family, however, knew nothing of these etymological and historical details: all they knew was that the lineage could be traced back to the humble little village of Llers. Once the painter became world-famous, a number of researchers searched through dusty records in parish archives, but to little avail. Dalí himself cooked up all manner of whimsical or fantastical explanations of the origin of his surname, which some biographers have dutifully recorded, but none of them have any value.

The artist's father was a very practical man who was not interested in knowing any more than that his ancestors were village blacksmiths, and that his father, Gal Dalí Vinyes, at the age of 31, had got rich with some business deal, had moved to Barcelona in 1881 with his wife and two sons, had started playing the stock market ... and had lost everything in the crisis of 1886. And had committed suicide, at the age of 36.

Gal's wife, Teresa Cusí, found herself a widow for the second time. With the two boys, she went to live at the home of the daughter she had had by her first marriage, who was married to Josep Maria Serraclara, a lawyer who was a member of the Republican Party and who would come to be a member of the powerful Barcelona City Council. Serraclara would become the protector of Teresa Cusí and her sons. The eldest of them, Salvador Dalí Cusí – that is, the artist's father – was thus able to graduate in law at the University of Barcelona and subsequently work in the lucrative Serraclara law firm.

On marrying Felipa Domènech in 1900, at the age of 29, Salvador Dalí Cusí could well believe that life was smiling on him, that they would have lots of children and live happily ever after.

Their first child, a boy named Salvador, came into the world in October 1901 and left it before the age of two. The second, also named Salvador after his dead brother, was born in May 1904 and became the spoiled and temperamental king of the house. The third and last child, born in 1908, was a girl, christened Anna Maria.

The life of the Dalís was that of an extended family, as it was for the vast majority of Catalan families of the time, however wealthy or modest. The traditional home was generally made up of parents, children, grandparents, aunts and uncles... Not only were households larger then than now, but each family had much closer links with their cousins, in-laws and other relations, and often the ties between cousins were stronger than between brothers and sisters. In addition, the towns and villages, where everyone knew everyone else, were the natural extension of the family circle, the arena for sociability, friendship, not to mention gossip and indiscretion.

The notary Salvador Dalí Cusí, with his solid build, dark hair and severe and sometimes defiant gaze, was proud of his importance in the town. A notary knew as much or even more about his fellow townspeople as the vicar did.

The authoritarian and short-tempered Mr. Dalí was very sure of himself, and gave everyone to understand that it was he who wore the trousers at home. He was traditional in his deeds but progressive in his ideas. Anti-clerical and anti-monarchic, like many people in Figueres, he was one of those Catalans who in café debates declared their support for a federal republic; who believed that Spain was a collection of diverse peoples that was culturally backward, dominated by a reactionary clergy and governed by brutish generals, crooked politicians and ignorant landowners. In contrast, the neighbouring French Republic was cultured home of individual liberties and the lay model to be emulated by the Catalan republicans. This explains why little Salvador Dalí, the future artist, was sent to a school run by French monks where all of the teaching was conducted in their own language.

At the age of ten, the young Salvador spoke and understood French fluently, more with the accent of the Midi than of Paris. He spoke nothing but Catalan with his family and friends. Many of the books, magazines and newspapers he leafed through were in Catalan. He would have had great difficulty in writing correctly even a single word of Castilian, the only language that was taught in the schools run by the Spanish state.

Absent-minded, fidgety and pensive, the son of the eminent notary Mr. Dalí was a poor student, one of those who would rather draw in the margins of their books than study the words printed there. At the age of 12 he began his secondary education at the state-run Municipal School of Figueres, where he went in the mornings, and at the school of the Marist Brothers (an order founded by the French priest M. Champagnat) in the afternoons.

The young Dalí's attention was captured, much more than by his school books, by a magazine, *En Patufet, ('The Tot')*. Written entirely in Catalan, it combined finely-illustrated tales with jokes and caricatures that amiably reflected everyday life. It had a circulation of over 60,000 and became the most popular publication for both young and old throughout Catalonia, employing first-rate writers and artists. From time to time the editors accepted outside collaborations, and in 1918 they published an impeccably-executed drawing by the 14-year-old Salvador Dalí: on the edge of a high clifftop, a boy is leaning dangerously over the edge, and his father, watching him from a few steps away, is sternly admonishing him, "Lad, I'm warning you, if you fall off I'll give you a good hiding!" Everyone laughed at the joke and admired the precocious artist's excellent line. Listening to the praise his son was receiving, Mr. Dalí began to think that the boy's passion for his pencil and paintbrush might be something more than a mere passing fancy after all.

The following year, after young Dalí took part in a collective exhibition of painting in Figueres, a journalist wrote in the local paper: "We salute the new artist and have the firm hope that, in times to come, our humble words

Pupils of the Marist Brothers' school in Figueres, academic year 1915-16. Inset, Salvador Dalí. (P)

will have the value of a prophecy: Salvador Dalí Domènech will be a great painter." To be considered a "great painter" in those days, one had to succeed in Paris … and the road that led there ran along the edge of the precipice.

CHAPTER 3

The Cabaret of Assassins

Paris, before the First World War

The *Cabaret des Assassins* was bursting with activity. It was a former farmhouse that stood beside the steep and poorly-cobbled road that led to the top of the hill of Montmartre.

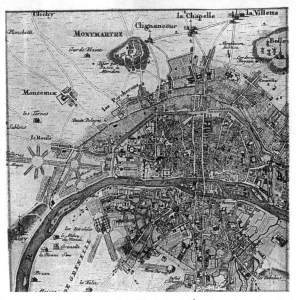

Montmartre in the second half of the 19th century, before being annexed to Paris.

The *Cabaret des Assassins* in Montmartre. Ink drawing by the Catalan artist Martí Vives. (AA)

In fact, the house had another name, but it was known as the *Cabaret of the Assassins* because it had become a tavern that looked more like a smoke-blackened cave, with macabre pictures and tools hung on its walls. One painting showed a madman slitting the throats of his own family. A blood-spattered knife was stuck into the wall beside it. The other pictures were in much the same general spirit.

And as for the clientele, apart from a couple of *filles de joie* and the customary louts and no-goods, the character of the joint was enlivened by a number of peculiar representatives of the city's cosmopolitan artistic bohemia: Wilhelm Apollinaris de Kostrowitzky, half-Polish, half-Italian, who had adopted the French name of Guillaume Apollinaire, wrote lascivious stories and poems and was obsessed with the Marquis de Sade and therefore with Sadism; the poet Max Jacob, a Breton Jew turned Catholic, whose works were at the same time mystical and burlesque; Francis Carco, real name Carcopino-Tusoli, a prose writer from the slums; Pierre Mac Orlan, real name Dumarchais, a painter and writer captivated by the rough underworld of port cities; Roland Lécavelé, real name Dorgelès, a novelist from Marseilles; and, among others, Pablo Picasso, real name Pablo Ruiz Picazo, an Andalusian painter who had trained in Barcelona.

It is true that Picasso and others patronised cabarets of a somewhat higher calibre in Montmartre, but nevertheless the whole district represented sin and vice for the civilised folk of the city. The Catalan merchant and writer Ferran Canyameres, who had been the patron of more than one bohemian artist and knew Paris well, was certainly not narrow-minded, but his description of the Montmartre of the early years of the 20th century is highly illustrative: "Montmartre had previously been a quiet little village, closed in by a wall which made it independent of Paris. Nearby there used to be taverns frequented by the riffraff. Many of them had obscene names and were little more than brothels, harbouring drunken orgies, covering up rape and murder ... When the city walls came down, Paris rushed in."

The bohemian artists rented workshops, rooms or houses in Montmartre. One of these houses, known as the 'Bateau-Lavoir', was Picasso's home for a time, and it was here, in 1906 and at the age of 26, that he left behind the naturalist painting that he had cultivated from a precocious age and began work on what is now considered to be the first Cubist painting, and which in its day must have caused a shock in every sense. It became known as *Les Demoiselles d'Avignon*, but its true title referred not to the French city but to Barcelona, for *Les senyoretes del carrer d'Avinyó* are the prostitutes of a brothel situated in the street of that name in the Catalan capital, an establishment Picasso knew well.

At that time, the pith-helmeted explorers of Europe's colonialist empires were discovering statuettes and masks of the sub-Saharan peoples, and *l'art noir* had become fashionable among the snobs of Paris. Following the trend, Picasso gave the faces of his prostitutes a certain negroid air. And, following the erratic attempts of his predecessor Cézanne, which were also partly inspired by primitive

27

African art forms, he gave the women square-shaped breasts. He represented their bodies schematically, deformed by unreal geometric volumes, and coloured them in muted ochre tomes on a background the colour of goose excrement, as can be appreciated in the exact place that corresponds to it: New York's Museum of Modern Art.

The period between 1907 and 1912 witnessed the explosion of the tumultuous phenomenon that came to be known as the artistic avant-garde.

At the end of the 19th century, Santiago Rusiñol, the Catalan artist who painted in the style of Degas, the Parisian Impressionist, could still allow himself to praise the beauty irradiated by the Cathedral of Notre Dame de Paris: "Sometimes we step into church of Notre Dame. What magic of harmony and what breath of genius gave birth to this forest of columns! What limbo of mysterious light! … It may be the tranquil dream state produced by the work of art, it may be the peace of the line, it may be something more that hovers around the areas of the temple. It is all of these at the same time, and something more that hums inside us, and it is an adoration for beautiful things."

A dozen years later, the iconoclastic critics of Paris, eager to *épater les bourgeois*, to shock the bourgeois classes, decreed that Impressionism was "old-fashioned." Their faithful acolytes in Barcelona, who always kept at least one eye on the French capital, swiftly repeated the *mot d'ordre* from Paris and announced with much ado that from now on what would be the rage would be the school of Cubism inaugurated by Picasso. The truth, the considerably silenced truth, is that Picasso's first Cubist painting did not even impress his friend Georges Braque, and much less the art dealers. The young ladies of Avinyó were put away in the artist's workshop and were only exhibited, timidly, to the public nine years later, when the avant-garde's breakthrough of the enemy lines had consolidated itself.

The torpedo into the flotation line of the vessel of traditional art was fired not by Picasso but by the impassioned

Italian-French writer Filippo Tommaso Marinetti, the brilliant ideologist of the movement which, shortly after the First World War, would adopt the name Futurism and be intimately linked to Fascism. The general outlines Marinetti had sketched out in the *Manifesto tecnico della letteratura futurista* (1912) were developed years later in *Patriottismo insetticida* (1939), *Canto eroico e machine della guerra mussoliniana* (1942) and *L'esercito italiana, poesia armata* (1942).

If Marinetti had set off his dialectical bomb in an Italian city it would have had little repercussion. However, he had not only the gift of language but also that of public relations, and in one way or another he got the founding text of the avant-garde published, on 22 February 1909, in the illustrious Parisian newspaper *Le Figaro*, the great organ of the bourgeoisie. The restless, unbridled prose of the *Manifeste de Futurisme* proclaimed:

"We intend to sing the love of danger, the habit of energy and fearlessness.

Courage, audacity, and revolt will be essential elements of our poetry.

Up to now literature has exalted a pensive immobility, ecstasy, and sleep. We intend to exalt aggressive action, a feverish insomnia, the racer's stride, the mortal leap, the punch and the slap.

We affirm that the world's magnificence has been enriched by a new beauty: the beauty of speed. A racing car whose hood is adorned with great pipes, like serpents of explosive breath – a roaring car that seems to ride on grapeshot is more beautiful than the *Victory of Samothrace*.

We want to hymn the man at the wheel, who hurls the lance of his spirit across the Earth, along the circle of its orbit.

The poet must spend himself with ardour, splendour, and generosity, to swell the enthusiastic fervour of the primordial elements.

Except in struggle, there is no more beauty. No work without an aggressive character can be a masterpiece.

Poetry must be conceived as a violent attack on unknown forces, to reduce and prostrate them before man.

We stand on the last promontory of the centuries! ... Why should we look back, when what we want is to break down the mysterious doors of the Impossible? Time and Space died yesterday. We already live in the absolute, because we have created eternal, omnipresent speed.

F.T. Marinetti, the founder of Futurism. (A)

We will glorify war – the world's only hygiene – militarism, patriotism, the destructive gesture of freedom-bringers, beautiful ideas worth dying for, and scorn for woman.

We will destroy the museums, libraries, academies of every kind, will fight moralism, feminism, every opportunistic or utilitarian cowardice."

The Italian Futurist movement was, undoubtedly, radical, but it bore in its bosom the indelible mark of its social origin, bourgeois bohemia. In Russia, on the other hand, Futurism found an outlet in the early years of the Communist movement.

CHAPTER 4

Inflammable mixture

Cadaqués (Catalonia), at the end of the First World War

The Spanish State had remained neutral during what the French called the *Grande Guerre*, later to be known as the First World War (1914-18). But the pictures and the vision of the slaughter of millions of young men on the killing fields of Europe had ploughed a deep furrow in the consciences of the European nations which stood aside from the disaster. From now on it would be so much more difficult to believe in the innate goodness of mankind, and as a result destructive, cynical, amoral, absurd or demented ideas would germinate more easily in the field of Western society that had been fertilised by the putrefying bodies of the unknown soldiers who had died *pour la patrie* – or for the 'beautiful ideas' proclaimed by Marinetti.

The conception of the artist as someone who delights in beauty and is capable of creating it would soon begin to splinter. One person who still believed in it was the 16-year-old Salvador Dalí, who, isolated in his family cocoon, wrote in one of his notebooks, "Manet, Degas, Renoir, the French Impressionists. It will be these who will guide my way most firmly!"

All Dalí knew of the French Impressionists at that time came from black-and-white prints reproducing their paintings and from the conversations of the old people of his clan in Figueres. Some members of the generation preceding Dalí's had even been able to see the paintings of the

31

French artists in real life, at an exhibition in Barcelona in 1907, on the occasion of the Fifth International Exposition held there. And like everything else that came from Paris, Impressionism had immediately been adopted, with greater or lesser success, by Catalan painters. One of them was Ramon Pichot, who happened to be a close friend of the notary Mr. Dalí. They were the same age, and they both spent the summers with their families at the houses they owned on the rugged, solitary beach of Cadaqués.

Pichot, an experienced artist who had trained in Paris, had painted in oils a view of a red-coloured bay, Cala Nans, overlooked in the foreground by a dark pine tree which contrasted with the bluish horizon and the yellowish clouds. The adolescent Dalí had imitated it, painting the same view, still with somewhat awkward strokes, with a similar composition but replacing the pine tree with a pair of cypresses.

Heirs of the great naturalistic pictorial tradition, based on a linear fidelity to nature and the construction on true perspective adopted by the Renaissance artists, the Impres-

Cala Nans, oil on canvas, 40 × 50 cm, in Impressionist style, painted by Dalí at the age of around 16. Private collection.

sionists tended to paint from life, as if taking a photograph of the chosen field of vision.

The composition of Impressionist paintings is rarely deceptive. The artists, with an instinctive sense of perspective, would distribute the volumes and boundaries in accordance with the classical canons, although they were beginning to be influenced by the new possibilities of framing used in photography. Whether painting indoors or *à plein air*, they tended to apply the rule of the 'golden section', which decrees that in order for a space divided into unequal parts to have a pleasant aesthetic effect, the same relationship must exist between the smaller part and the larger as between the larger part and the whole. On this standard structure, the colours were applied: warm tones which create a sensation of nearness in the foreground, and cool tones in the middle and background to heighten the impression of distance.

The brush stroke, in general, was quick and short. What largely distinguished the Impressionists from other pictorial schools was that instead of creating a painstakingly detailed representation of landscapes, objects or persons, they aimed to evoke a sensation, an "impression" of the true ephemerality of vision. The shimmering patch of sunlight that suddenly imbues a dark corner with life; the wind that constantly changes the outlines of clouds and trees; the crest of the waves sparkling in the bay; the movement of the dance that makes the girls' skirts fly; the fleetingness of life itself.

From the age of 14 until shortly before turning 22, Dalí painted several pictures in gouache on board, watercolours, Chinese ink and, especially, oils. Most of them were drawn or painted during the long summers in Cadaqués. Examined closely, these paintings are seen to be the erratic attempts of a young artist full of confused ideas who is searching for his own style by imitating others. If there had been any club at the time willing to admit him, it could only have been the club, now teeming with members, of those whose motto is "We don't know where we're going, but we're going there with absolute determination!"

The oil painting *Vell crepuscular* (*Old Man at Dusk*, private collection), which Dalí created at the age of 14, catches the attention through the force of its brush strokes, scattered wildly around a hunchbacked old man looming gigantically before a cove whose pale waters reflect the shifting reddish light of dusk.

Between the ages of 14 and 16 he painted a *Self-Portrait* in oils which is a prized possession of the Salvador Dalí Museum in Saint Petersburg, Florida. The simple composition rests on just four lines drawn in pencil. Through the open door of an old fisherman's house, which fills up over a third of the canvas, there enters the daylight, illuminating the easel and the back of the artist, who is sitting in a rush-bottomed chair, typical of Catalan rural homes. The artist's position is unrealistic, because the light enters from the right and would therefore throw the shadow of the painter's hand onto the canvas. But the artist was not interested in realism, but the explosion of light into a dim room. The interior walls and the pair of chairs are painted in Prussian blue, and the doors, the floor, the easel, the illuminated part of the floor and even the artist's trousers in vermilion, and the whole forms a pleasing chromatic blend. This picture is more a rapid sketch than a finished painting, but it is sufficient to reveal the energetic stroke, the apt choice of colour and the passionate excitement of the painter attempting to produce a canvas in the manner of the Impressionists.

Another oil painting, of the sailing boat '*El Son*' (Figueres Museum), produced at the age of 15, shows greater certainty in construction and in the placement of touches of colour. The stroke continues to be rustic, but it is the rusticity of a mind which is clearly gifted for painting, not that of a mere *naïf* lacking in artistic sense.

The spongelike mind of the young Dalí effortlessly absorbed any pictorial model placed before it. At 17, he did a pair of gouache paintings on board representing cheerful scenes of the traditional fairs of Figueres. The execution of the coloured drawings is excellent, but it is no longer the style of the Impressionists; it is a different, expressionistic style which had been made fashionable by the Catalan artist Xavier Nogués.

In 1951, one of Dalí's contemporaries and a fellow native of Figueres, the delicate symbolist poet Jaume Maurici i Soler, wrote some truthful memoirs about the youthful artist which tend to be omitted by the biographers who only highlight the scandalous life and work of the Surrealist adult Dalí. "Dalí must have been sixteen or seventeen then," wrote Maurici. "I remember the visit my friend Joan Subias and I made to his workshop in Figueres. It was a pleasant evening, with the last light of the afternoon falling on the palm tree in the neighbouring square. It was the first time we had spoken to Dalí. He showed us his first oil paintings. They reflected the cobalt of the sea of Cadaqués and the greyish tones of the surrounding hills. An endless sky covered the whole. I remember that I then published my impressions of them in a modest weekly publication of Figueres, and this perhaps opened the gates for the immense amount of print our genial painter has generated. In my mind I still retain an indelible impression of that first contact with a Dalí who was almost timid, with great natural distinction, practically diffident, without a trace of pretension or vanity. Ever since then I have carried with me *my* Dalí, the one who has not been overcome by this other Dalí of Surrealism, the Dalí of his sister Anna Maria..."

In this testimony, the delicate Maurici merely suggests the great love that Anna Maria Dalí felt for her brother. It seems that this love went in just one direction and beyond an affection between siblings. Within the old families of Cadaqués it used to be said that Anna Maria was a sexually liberated girl who was extremely attracted by masculine beauty and considered sexual relationships something as natural as all the other bodily functions.

In the same period, in 1921, Dalí produced an unsettling *Self-Portrait* which is also now in the Salvador Dalí Museum in Saint Petersburg, Florida. It emanates a disconcerting, morbid air. In the icy, inhuman gaze of the self-portrayed artist we perceive something sickly, a shadow of perversity. Something was not right in the Dalí home.

In the February of that year of 1921, after months of suffering, Dalí's mother Felipa had died at the age of 47 – of cancer, it has been written. What has not been told is what the Dalís' neighbours knew but did not spread: that Felipa suffered from a serious mental illness, which obviously helps to explain the crazy life of her son the artist. The premature death of Felipa, who perhaps had never recovered from the death of her first child, must have shaken all of the family. And Felipa's own mother, grandmother Anna Maria, remained distressed by the experience until her own death twenty months later.

Some twenty years later, in his book *The Secret Life of Salvador Dalí*, the artist himself evoked his mother's death in baroque rhetoric: "In the middle of my chest I felt the gigantic branches of the millenary cedar of Lebanon of revenge spreading. With my teeth worn jagged by so much weeping, I swore to myself that I would tear my mother from death with the swords of light that would one day shine around my glorious name."

Something deeper than the publicity-styled prose of this text must have lain concealed in Dalí's soul. Oddly, it is not sorrow, nor pain, nor anguish, nor melancholy, nor anything similar that is reflected in the 1921 self-portrait, but an unsettling distancing from the rest of humanity. The first person to sense a complex, conflictive undertow in Dalí's personality had to be his mother. How she took it, and the suffering it brought her, are secrets she carried to her grave.

Dalí's father remarried – with Felipa's sister, Caterina, who lived with the family. And the days, months and seasons passed, between Figueres and Cadaqués, with the indifference they had always shown.

Nothing deterred the single-minded Salvador Dalí from painting. In 1922 he had entered the Academy of San Fernando art school in Madrid, and was living at the city's Students' Residence, where he struck up a friendship with a young Andalusian poet, Federico García Lorca, and a film student from Aragon called Luis Buñuel. In 1923 Dalí was expelled from the school for insulting two teachers. He returned home, swallowed his frustration and his father's ill-humour and shut himself in his studio to paint, and at the end of the year he enrolled in another Madrid school, the Free Academy, naturally at his father's expense.

García Lorca (left) with Dalí, in military uniform, in Figueres. (FD)

In 1924, Mr. Dalí the notary, well-known for his liberal ideas, came into conflict with the authorities of Spain's recently-installed military dictatorship. Whether it was to pressurise the father, or because the son was found in possession of some leaflets considered 'subversive', or for some other reason, the fact is that the 19-year-old Salvador Dalí was arrested and imprisoned for over a month. He recovered, perhaps, from this experience during a holiday in Cadaqués in 1925, accompanied by his close friend Lorca, whose homosexuality provoked comments of all kinds.

In any case, the artist's sister Anna Maria always had good memories of that time: "The smart appearance Salvador had acquired in Madrid continued. His suits were elegant and impeccable, he combed his hair carefully and his whole person gave off an air of serenity and well-being. He was methodical in his work and would read a lot. The book he never put down was Ingres' *Les Pensées*. The catalogue of the exhibition Dalí Salvador held in Barcelona [from 14 to 27 November 1925] contains three of Ingres' thoughts on painting which perhaps sum up the concept he had of it then, as follows:

'Drawing is the probity of art.'

'He who aims to contribute no spirit other than his own will soon find himself reduced to the most wretched of imitations, that is, to that of his own works.'

'The beautiful forms are erect planes with rounded shapes. The beautiful forms are those which have firmness and fullness, in which the details do not compromise the appearance of the large masses.'

In January 1926, Dalí exhibited some of his work in Madrid. In April, during the Easter holidays, he travelled to Paris for the first time. Although he was about to turn 22, he did not go alone or with friends, but with his aunt (and stepmother) Caterina and his sister Anna Maria. The spoilt child of the house was well escorted.

"The main reason for the trip to Paris," Anna Maria said later, "was to visit the Louvre Museum. The artists that

Pòrtic de Ventura Gassol

Dalí illustrated the cover of the book *Les bruixes de Llers,* by C. Fages de Climent, with a prologue by Ventura Gassol, in 1925. (AA)

most attracted my brother's attention were Leonardo da Vinci, Raphael and Ingres. He stood, literally, in ecstasy before the work of these artists. He also felt a great interest for the Flemish painters, and so we went to Belgium to study them, particularly Vermeer's pictures of Delft. Thanks to that journey, he was finally able to admire the originals of the paintings that all through his childhood he had never tired of gazing at in the pages of *Gowans* [an illustrated publication of the time]."

In the French capital, Dalí made a superficial acquaintance with Picasso, then aged 45. He also met up again with

Luis Buñuel, his ex-classmate from Madrid, who was working as an assistant to the French filmmaker Jean Epstein.

For any Catalan, of whatever nature or status, going to Paris in those days was equivalent to going to the capital of Europe, and this privilege illuminated the person with a special light in the eyes of his or her envious compatriots. For an artist, or for someone aiming to become one, it was the Mecca of the arts. For Dalí it was the first step on the way to conquering the world.

In his personal diary, some pages of which are conserved in Figueres, the 16-year-old artist had written in black ink, "I will be a genius and the world will admire me." For the moment, he was gaining success back in Barcelona. His perceptive sister Anna Maria, who had chastely served as a model for many of Dalí's pictures, recalls it this way: "We were preparing the second exhibition at the Galeries Dalmau in Barcelona, which took place from 31 December 1926 to 14 January 1927. Salvador showed, among others, the following paintings: *Anna Maria* (paint on copper); *Study for the picture Anna Maria*; another *Study for the picture Anna Maria*; *Girl with Curls*; *Girl Sewing*; *Basket of Bread*; *Girl in the Window*; *Rocks of El Llaner*; *Cliffs*; and *Venus and Cupid*. I mention these pictures because they are the most important of that period. They reflect a healthy, classical, brilliant soul..."

Overlooking the paintings that were beginning to cause the family more than a little embarrassment, Anna Maria Dalí chose these pictures with the legitimate pride of knowing she was the protagonist of most of them, but also with the accurate conviction that they were the only ones that appealed to almost everyone. The fact is that these canvases have been admired by virtually everyone who has ever seen them, and there is no shortage of critics who, in *Basket of Bread* and *Girl in the Window*, have seen masterpieces.

One fact that tends to be silenced by art critics more interested in the erotic aspects of Dalí's art is that the realistic bread baskets he painted before the year 1928, which could easily pass for the work of some highly skilled Dutch painter of the 17th century, were irrefutable proof of Dalí's extraordinary technical prowess. This was appreciated not only by the Catalan art critics of the 1920's but also by the general public, perhaps inexperienced in art but fully endowed with perception and judgement, who were able to admire the loaves and their baskets in photographic reproductions illustrating the popular calendars that hung on the walls of the shops and homes of both the middle and working classes.

Among the Catalan public, Dalí's fame as a great painter was gained not through the later Surrealist and macabre works – which were unknown to the great majority – but by that bread basket, more perfect than a photograph, and that 'daily bread' everyone had to earn with the sweat of their brow, that bread that was so scarce during and after the Spanish Civil War. One of those pictures of bread baskets was soon on its way to the USA, an event recalled by Anna Maria Dalí, who witnessed it herself.

"The success of that exhibition attracted attention from abroad. A delegate of the Carnegie Institute in Pittsburgh, Pennsylvania, came to Figueres to buy two paintings for the Pittsburgh Museum of Modern Art. He bought the *Basket of Bread*, and if he didn't walk off with the picture entitled *Anna Maria* it was because my father didn't want to sell it, as it was a portrait of me. There were dealers from Paris who came to Figueres, too…"

The young painter often portrayed his father and sister. Once he also painted his maternal grandmother, Maria Anna Ferrés, as she sewed in front of the window. In his imagination, Salvador Dalí dreamed of devouring the whole world, but the umbilical cord that bound him to his family and his home territory was immensely tight and strong. The Empordà region is notorious for its *tramuntana*, the persistent, maddening wind from over the Pyrenees, and on days when it was blowing, the fanciful young

Photograph of Cadaqués in the 1920's. (AA)

painter could easily envisage fantastical, malignant figures swirling around in the clouds scudding across the bay of Cadaqués. But that piece of sky was also a familiar and protective shield.

Cadaqués is dominated to the south-west by a range of hills rising abruptly to over 600 metres of altitude, and screened to the north-east by another arc of hills. As a result, until a heavily winding road was built through the hills at the end of the 19th century, the town's only truly practical access was by sea. Anna Maria Dalí knew old fishermen who in their youth had sailed to Genoa, Marseilles, even Cuba and Tierra del Fuego, but had never set foot in Figueres.

Geographical isolation led, naturally, to endogamy in human relationships. One member of the Pichot clan had married his own aunt. Gal Dalí Vinyes himself, the artist's paternal grandfather, had married a distant relative whose

42

second (maternal) surname was also Vinyes. When Salvador's mother died, his father married her sister, who moreover had always lived with them. And in Cadaqués in particular, everything stayed in the family, including the possibility of habitual marriage between close relatives producing backward children and grandchildren. But even in that tightly-closed little yard, the seed of the wild oats of the big city could still take root. On recalling the exhibition at the Galeries Dalmau, Anna Maria Dalí added that her brother's "healthy, classical, brilliant soul ... would soon be tarnished by the breath of Surrealism."

A born imitator, Dalí had glimpsed the possibility, during his stay in Paris, that by turning his back on classical painting he could channel the sickly manias that tormented him into avant-garde forms of expression. Surrealism had flourished in Paris, and not by spontaneous generation. Its roots fed on an earlier "-ism" of longer and wider extension: Futurism.

Dalí's swing to Surrealism was propitiated by the arrival in Barcelona, in February, of Marinetti, then aged 50, a tall, elegant, quite athletic figure who showed off a phenomenal black moustache with upended points. Marinetti, who sang to war as the *unica igiene nel mondo* and propounded the search for the absurd and the impossible, declared that Dalí was one of his followers.

With this letter of introduction from the Italian agitator – if, indeed, he really needed it – Salvador Dalí could now breeze through the opened doors of the restricted club of the Surrealist provocateurs. Preaching absurdity and the subversion of morals and taste, they claimed to be practising an art more real than reality itself: hence the name, originally coined in French, *Surréalisme*, 'over-realism'.

The members of this club preached by example. One of its members, Marcel Duchamp, had made a name for himself by presenting a significant work: a piece of pottery so real that the 'artist' had simply bought it in his local

43

sanitary fittings shop and then painted his signature on it. It was a urinal, as installed in public lavatories. "A bluff," the art critics of the great traditional newspapers hastened to proclaim. But perhaps it was not entirely a bluff. The first *Manifeste de Surréalisme*, published by the poet André Breton in 1924, was subtitled '*poison soluble*', soluble poison. And Salvador Dalí immediately saw that from the toxic reek of the Surrealists' urinals, mixed with the stench of gunpowder so beloved to the Futurists, someone could make an inflammable mixture. And that someone would be him, and the resulting explosion would project him into the clouds. They would say he was a genius and the world would admire him ... perhaps.

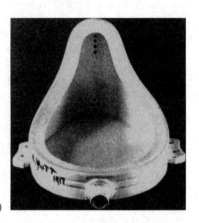

Duchamp's urinal. (GSM)

PART TWO

CHAPTER 5

The roses of the desert

Madrid, 1920's

Struggling with a large suitcase, a slightly timid Dalí entered the Students' Residence in Madrid one day in September 1922. His prudent father believed that an artist who had to rely purely on selling his work was likely to have a hard time making a living, but being able to work as an art teacher with an official qualification was quite a different matter. So he decided to send his son to study painting at the Academy of San Fernando in the Spanish capital, not for the quality of its teaching, which he knew nothing about, but because in a centralist state like Spain any diploma bearing the name of the capital quickly rose to the top of the heap. Moreover, Salvador could live at the Students' Residence, which was known, and perhaps justifiably, as an oasis of cultured, modern minds in the heart of the decadent cultural wasteland of Castile. The Residence had been the home of the eminent philosopher José Ortega y Gasset (Castilian on his father's side and of distant Catalan origins on his mother's), and a number of illustrious European figures had spent time there, such as the German philosopher Count von Keyserling, the inimitable English writer G.K. Chesterton, the French novelist François Mauriac, the Polish-French physicist Marie Curie and the Russian composer Igor Stravinsky.

In Madrid, separated from Figueres by some 700 kilometres, Salvador Dalí was beginning his first long stay away

47

from home. After undergoing the customary humiliating tricks the veteran residents inflicted on newcomers and which recalled and derived from the initiation rites into maturity of primitive peoples, the young males, temporarily removed from the restrictions and taboos imposed by life in the family and the home community, formed groups based on their various affinities. And if there was one common curiosity that united them all, it was the sexual instinct in permanent erection.

True, the geographical setting in this case was not a jungle teeming with wild animals but the remote Castilian capital, isolated on its vast, treeless plateau, populated mainly by functionaries and servants, totalling some 875,000 souls including the King, who lived in the Royal Palace. The anthropologist Julio Caro Baroja had described the Madrid of the time with vividly-coloured scenes such as ox-carts trundling along the streets loaded with bushes for the bakers' ovens. The doorways of the aristocrats' mansions were manned by uniformed doormen and tailcoated butlers, and on the street corners it was common to see blind beggars singing ballads, while soldiers in red and blue uniforms strolled alongside dressmakers, nurses and maids.

"I don't miss those concierges' cubby-holes that smelled of lavender mixed with cat's piss, nor the debates in neighbourhood cafés," said Caro Baroja, who, whenever he saw a man in a peaked cap and dark blue shirt, would take him to be one of the few more-or-less socialist typesetters of the few impoverished printing works, which disseminated a literature which was mostly of purely local interest but which, thanks to being published in the capital of the state, acquired an aura of importance in the backward provinces. A certain Mr. Gómez de la Serna, who had the physical defect of being as short as a dwarf and who made plays on words in the Dada style (a short-lived avant-garde aesthetic trend), was considered in Madrid to be the most modern of writers, but among the more enlightened writers from

48

outside the capital he amounted to little. The Catalan writer Josep Pla, a fellow Empordà native of Dalí, a foreign correspondent and a true man of letters, said: "I met this Mr. Gómez de la Serna at the Café Pombo in Calle Carretas in Madrid. For all the publicity this café has received, I found it as banal as could be. This gentleman was a pigmy, with a big head topped by a pretentious toupee. He was amusing when he talked, but when he wrote he was unintelligible, and, as he himself said, his favourite paper for writing was a roll of toilet paper. In reality, this writer is a purely fictitious phenomenon."

Dalí, at 18, was gifted with sharp intelligence and a lively imagination, but he was still uncertain in the foreign territory he was now treading, and he quickly teamed up with a number of older colleagues at the Students' Residence with whom he could share similar ideas, tendencies or obsessions to his own and on the same level of intelligence: among them, Federico García Lorca, Luis Buñuel and Eugenio Montes.

According to all of the indications, Lorca, who was six years older than Dalí, attempted, apparently unsucces-

Luis Buñuel as seen by Dalí. Oil on canvas, 59 × 69 cm, 1924.

sfully, to initiate him into the game of homosexual insinu-ations, fantasies and caresses. Buñuel, who was four years older, shocked Dalí with his destructive, pornographic ideas and aroused in him an interest in the silent cinema. In Eugenio Montes, seven years older, Dalí saw a cultured writer, the propagandist of a Castile-based Hispanic literary application of the ideas of Cubism and Italian Futurism.

Dalí wrote in an ugly hand that was at times horrifying, and he blithely broke all the rules of grammar, whether in French, Catalan or Spanish. On the other hand, he had great facility in expressing himself in writing, even if it was to express a chaotic line of argument, and he admired both the direct style of Marinetti and the precious manne-risms of Montes.

Despite his eventful student career at the art schools in Madrid, not to mention other obstacles, Dalí never stopped painting nor surprising those who paid attention to him. His expulsion from the Academy of San Fernando at the age of 19 contributed to creating his fame as a rebellious artist in the listless artistic circles of the capital, while his imprisonment in the military headquarters in Figueres at the age of 20 helped to establish his name among his townsfolk.

By the time he exhibited a series of paintings in Madrid in January 1926, the name of Salvador Dalí was no longer that of an unknown. And when, that autumn, he exhibited paintings in Barcelona beside the avant-garde canvases of Delaunay, Dufy, Picabia and Miró, both the art critics and the press of Catalonia and Madrid gave ample coverage to the event.

In February 1927, about to turn 23, he had to return to the castle of Figueres to begin his compulsory military service. But thanks to his father's influence he had to fulfil only a minimum of requirements, even though Spain was by then under a military dictatorship. As the moral calibre of the professional soldiers resembled more the Mexican irregulars of Pancho Villa than the Prussian generals, the

gift of a case of Havana cigars to the brigadier could somewhat alleviate the life of a common soldier. And a discreet
conversation between the notary Mr. Dalí and the colonel
could enable the soldier to spend more time outside the
barracks than inside. Both the notary and the colonel were
functionaries of the State, and moreover, as in the banana
republics, no-one knew when the political winds might
suddenly turn; and if they did turn, power would almost
certainly return to the notary's allies and associates, and
old favours and denials would surely be remembered.

In the circumstances, then, the notary's son was able to
dedicate almost all of his time to the world of art, just when
it was suffering a feverish commotion.

In 1924, the French writer André Breton, an admirer of
the Bolsheviks, published in Paris his *Manifeste de Surréalisme*. Shortly afterwards, Marinetti published in Rome his
Futurismo e fascismo, a proclamation which supplied a cohe-
rent ideology to the *Fasci di combattimento*, the shock troops
created by Mussolini.

One intellectual who was dazzled by the work and personality of Dalí was Ernesto Giménez Caballero, a leading figure in the adoption of futurism in Madrid and one of the
suppliers of ideological oxygen to the then embryonic Fascist movement in Castile and Spain in general. Giménez
Caballero, a dark, thin individual with a contemptuous air
and great intelligence, was five years older than Dalí. He
was the son of a Madrid printer and had worked as a type-
setter in his workshop, where he had developed a passion
for reading. He had founded the magazine *La Gaceta Literaria* and had made himself known as a writer of blasphemous tavern-style anecdotes with the booklet *Yo, inspector de alcantarillas* (*I, Inspector of Sewers*).

In another book, *Julepe de menta* (*Mint Julep*), published
in 1929, Giménez Caballero, who had made frequent visits
to Italy, wrote:

"It is plain that with eighteen years of Futurism, there
were few, in fact, who had taken serious notice [in Madrid]

Ernesto Giménez Caballero, publisher of *La Gaceta Literaria*. Drawing by L. García, 1929. (AA)

of the Italian avant-garde movement. Moreover, Marinetti has not received great appreciation. *ABC* and other Madrid newspapers cannot forget that Marinetti was an anti-clerical, an anti-academic and a revolutionary. Only *La Gaceta Literaria*, which I have the pleasure of directing, paid literary tribute to Marinetti without concerning itself about the political consequences. Or rather, concerning itself greatly. Because the opinion of its publisher – that is, my own – is that we must intensify the bonds of friendship and intelligence between the Spanish and Italian peoples ... in order for the two nations to manoeuvre jointly against the Anglo-Saxon arch-enemy, a millenary enemy who is today reviving voraciously on the American continent, threatening the Romanic, Hispano-Italian America ... Collaboration has to be the future task of our two great nations on the road to freeing ourselves from Nordic interference, from false, blond-haired liberalisms."

Everything that came out of Fascist Italy, like every irrational, incoherent, asystemic, destructive expression and everything smelling of revolution, whether Fascist or Bolshevik, it made no difference, quickly found a place in the mind of Giménez Caballero and the pages of his magazine.

(Nine years later, in the closing stages of the Spanish Civil War, and safely installed in Francoist territory, he would write: "From *La Gaceta Literaria* emerged the two spiritual [*sic*] youth movements which have solidified the future of Spain: the Communists and the Fascists.")

The fact is that when he met Dalí in the autumn of 1927, the publisher of *La Gaceta Literaria* realised that the excesses of the Catalan painter could boost the publication's sales, and he hastened to invite him to write for it. Dalí was equally quick to accept.

At that time, Dalí's friend Luis Buñuel was working in Paris, assisting the cineaste Jean Epstein in filming *La chute de la maison d'Usher* (*The Fall of the House of Usher*), based on the macabre tale by Edgar Allan Poe. Buñuel became another ideal collaborator of *La Gaceta Literaria*, as its cinema correspondent in the French capital.

Giménez Caballero had a film camera at home, and he attempted to imitate the spasmodic experiments then being made by the avant-garde filmmakers in Paris, Germany and Russia. As a result, when Dalí proposed to Buñuel a heap of bizarre ideas for a film to be entitled *Un chien andalou* (*An Andalusian Dog*), Giménez Caballero pricked up his ears and asked Dalí to show him the script. It was no more than a jumble of tangled ideas, but it contained enough shrapnel for the publisher to rush to the printing press and make a big splash of it in the *Gaceta Literaria* of 1 February 1929.

This short silent film, of just 17 minutes, was made with the 25,000 pesetas that Buñuel's mother had left her son. In the opening scene, a man's hands are sharpening a barber's razor; a woman's head rests against the man's chest as if he were about to shave her, but what he does is raise her eyelid, press the blade against her eyeball and, in ferocious close-up, slit it open.

Another sequence shows a hand (Dalí's) trying to touch a girl, but restrained by two ropes being dragged across the ground by two Marist brothers dressed in their typical black cassocks and round hats, followed by two pianos on which lie the rotting bodies of two asses. One of the actors is Dalí himself, and the other is one of his friends from Figueres, the journalist Jaume ('Met') Miravitlles.

In another scene, a hand is trapped between a door and the wall; the close-up reveals a horde of ants feeding on the fingers and palm. And in the final scene, the last of the horrors: two individuals buried in the sand up to their chests are slowly being devoured by a mass of insects, while superimposed in the background there appears the expression '*au printemps...*' ('in the spring...')

The Paris correspondent of the Catalan magazine *D'Ací i d'Allà*, whose prime concern was always to be *à la page*, reported that the select audience at the premiere included Louis Aragon, Hans Arp, Constantin Brancusi, André Breton, René Clair, Le Corbusier, Robert Desnos, Max Ernst, Jacques Lipschitz, Viscount Charles de Noailles and his wife Marie-Laure, Man Ray, E. Tériade, Tristan Tzara, Roger Vildrac and Christian Zervos.

The illustrious Viscount and Viscountess de Noailles apparently shared the poet Apollinaire's fascination with Sadism, and they were so electrified by the film that they offered Buñuel and Dalí the funds to make another film as exciting as this first one. According to the *Gran Enciclopèdia Catalana*, it was Marie-Laure de Noailles' money, inherited from her American banker father Maurice Bischoffsheim, which financed Buñuel and Dalí's second film, entitled *L'âge d'or* (*The Golden Age*).

Another person captivated by *Un chien andalou* was Buñuel and Dalí's former colleague from the Student's Residence in Madrid, Eugenio Montes, who wrote an original tribute to it in *La Gaceta*, for reasons quite different from, but not incompatible with, those of the De Noailles. Montes, in his nostalgia for Spain's lost empire, was especially struck by the fact that the commotion caused by *Un chien andalou* in the French capital was due to two Spanish men, the Aragonese Buñuel and the Catalan Dalí. Montes described it as if the French intelligentsia had thrown themselves at the feet of the two Spanish artists in much the same way as the Dutch surrender to the Spanish army at Breda in 1625, as if it were a triumph of the eternal but now barren Spain over the florid Versaillesque gardens of France. And playing on the idea of the "beauty" of spilt blood, he alluded to the processions of baroque images of Christ during Easter Week in Spain, particularly in Andalusia and Castile, marching solemnly through narrow streets to the military beat of drums, escorted by rifle-bearing troops of the Civil Guard.

Montes wrote: "Buñuel and Dalí have decidedly set themselves apart from what calls itself good taste, what is pleasant, agreeable, skin-deep, what is called *French*. A phonograph accompanied the film with the music from *Tristan and Isolde*. But what it should have played is the *jota* [the typical Aragonese folk dance] of that woman who refused to be French, who wanted to be Aragonese, from Spain and from the Ebro, this Iberian Nile (Aragon, you are an Egypt and you raise up pyramids of *jotas* to death). The barbaric, elementary beauty of the moon, the earth of the desert where blood is sweeter than honey, is finally reappearing in the world. No, do not seek the roses of France. Spain is not a garden, nor are the Spanish gardeners. Spain is a planet where the roses are rotting asses. It wants nothing of the spirit, nothing of decoration. Spain is the monastery of El Escorial, not refinement, because she can falsify nothing. In Spain, the Christs nailed to the cross pour blood, and when they are taken into the streets for the processions, they march between two lines of Civil Guard … *Un chien andalou* is a date in the history of the cinema, a date marked with blood, as Nietzsche wanted it, as Spain has always done…"

CHAPTER 6

The evidence of the crime

Cadaqués, summer 1929

The odd couple disembarked in Cadaqués one day in the summer of 1929. He was *monsieur* Eugène Grindel, a refined Parisian of 33. She, *madame* Grindel, was, according to Max Ernst's biographer Patrick Waldberg, "an energetic, seductive, even aggressive woman, with charming manners and an intense, penetrating gaze." The French she spoke was not that nasal dialect of the educated Parisian classes who, when they say "Bonjour", feel obliged to form a perfect circle with the lips; no, her French was full of sharp, open vowels, an accent at once vulgar and exotic.

M Grindel was the son of a humble accountant married to a seamstress, who, in the years of brutal speculation preceding Paris's Universal Exposition of 1889, symbolised by the building of the Eiffel Tower, had managed to take advantage of certain obscure financial operations to make himself a fortune.

Mme Grindel, understood to be of Russian parentage, had emigrated to Paris, leaving behind her mother, Antoinette, now with a second husband of whom little or nothing is known for certain. This exotic woman, born into the Russian Orthodox Church, had married M Grindel at a Catholic ceremony in 1917, after they met at a sanatorium in Davos, Switzerland, when they were both convalescing from tuberculosis. The following year, the marriage had produced a daughter, Cécile, who was now with her parents

56

in Cadaqués at the invitation of the artist Salvador Dalí, along with other acquaintances of his.

But things were not qute as clear-cut as this. M Eugène-Émile-Paul Grindel was now calling himself Paul Éluard, and this was the name he used to sign the *pensées* he passed off as poems. Mme Grindel made herself known as Gala, although her true name is a mystery, or at best a muddle. Meryle Secrest, an American author who wrote a biography of Dalí, calls her Helena (or Elena) Deluvina Diakonoff, the surname being either her father's or her stepfather's. (Secrest believes the stepfather was Jewish, a suggestion Gala could not bear to listen to.) The first edition of the *Gran Enciclopèdia Catalana*, published in 1974, named her Gala Dianaroff. In Dalí's last will and testament dated 12 December 1980, the Barcelona notary Ramon Coll Figa recorded her name as Elena Diakanoff de Ullina. And to clarify things still further, the Irish Hispanist Ian Gibson, in his biography of Dalí published in London in 1997, calls her Helena Ivánovna Diákonova. All this confusion merely serves to reinforce the first impression: that the lady's true origins are not at all clearly known to us.

According to her own will, Gala was born in Kazan, a large walled city on the Volga, the capital of the Tatar people of Turco-Mongolian descent, whose country had been annexed by Russia in the 16th century. Gala had been educated in Saint Petersburg, and she spoke and wrote in Russian and French.

The couple formed by Éluard and Gala was certainly not the type of couple the people of Cadaqués were used to seeing. Just a few years after marrying, they had formed a *ménage à trois* by sharing their bed in Paris with Max Ernst, a German artist who suffered from mental disorders which, instead of being diminished by his psychiatric studies, had in some way come to imbue his paintings. This *ménage à trois* had ended in blows between the two men. The German found another woman for company, but the relationship between Éluard and Gala was never the same again. This became plain in Cadaqués at the end of the summer, as they prepared to return to Paris with the other companions: Buñuel, the enigmatic Walloon painter René Magritte and the Flemish art dealer Camille Goemans. They all set off for the French capital, accompanying Éluard and his daughter Cécile. But Gala stayed behind in Cadaqués with Dalí.

The effect on the Dalí family of the contact with this Parisian troupe was related by the artist's sister, Anna Maria, in this way:

Portrait of Gala, 1927.
(A)

"That summer was enough to exert on my brother the change that distanced him from his friends, from us and from himself ... under the pressure of those complicated beings ... The brilliance of the mica of the rocks, the dazzle of the sun on the sea, the silver leaves of the olive trees, everything trembled with fear under the red-eyed gaze of those strange characters who did not appreciate the treasure of the tenderness of the lights of our fishing village. Their eagerness to destroy the bases that form the morality and goodness of human beings was so fanatical that their indignation reached a limit when, for one moment, they glimpsed a good and pure world that was opposed to theirs. It seemed impossible that my brother could be

58

dragged along by them, but that is what happened ... He lost his peace of mind and that well-being that his works had reflected until then. The pictures he was painting now were horribly hallucinatory. He was sculpting true nightmares on his canvases. Disturbing, tortured figures that seemed to tell of inexplicable things, those things that, as in dreams, you seem to understand when you see them but then leave only the memory of a hallucination. *Le jeu lugubre* is the most vivid representation of that time...

"But time was moving towards a new tragedy. We could see that Salvador's mind was being dominated by those amoral beings, and we understood that no good would come of it. My father was seriously worried. His bright, kind eyes now stared fixedly as if he was trying to chase after the thoughts that came to him, dense and dark like storm clouds. He twisted his white hair, a clear sign in him of great concern, and his face, usually optimistic and smiling, showed a fear of some tragic outcome."

In the few weeks that Éluard's wife spent in Cadaqués, Dalí's behaviour underwent a sudden and profound change that a less kindly and more objective eye than his sister's might well have foreseen on inspecting the self-portrait the artist produced at the age of 17 and, in particular, on viewing *Un chien andalou.*

Gala was probably the first woman Dalí had gone to bed with; the first woman to satisfy him sexually; the first woman to exert a profound domination over him since the death of his mother. All of those who knew Dalí then and have spoken about it coincide in the exaltation, the passion, the frantic activity and shamelessness shown by him at that time. All of the inflammable material stored in Dalí's debauched mind since his childhood was now exploding.

We do not know what happens, and why, in the deepest reaches of the mind. Episodes of psychosis and paranoia appear and disappear for reasons that psychiatry cannot explain. We have to limit ourselves to observing that, at certain moments, an extremely sensitive individual reacts

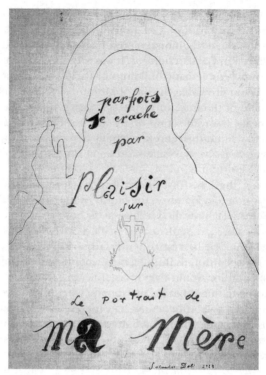

Parfois je crache par plaisir sur le portrait de ma mère, also entitled *The Sacred Heart*. Ink on canvas, 68 × 50 cm, 1929.

with a behaviour which does not seem to obey any logic. "He's gone mad" or "She's half crazy" are habitual popular expressions for this phenomenon. Dalí, who was filling his canvases with fearful obsessions, suddenly manifested an unexpected abscess of hate towards his mother, who had died eight years earlier.

At the end of 1929, Goemans' art gallery in Paris exhibited twelve disturbing pictures by Dalí. All of them were very carefully worked, except for one which was not a painting but an ink drawing of the silhouette of the Sacred Heart of Jesus, a traditional pious image that was very commonly seen in Catalan homes. (It was also the name of one of the most emblematic buildings of Paris, the Temple du Sacré-Coeur crowning the hill of Montmartre.) Occupying the whole of the interior of the silhouette, and in writing that recalls the wild scrawl of certain psychiatric patients, Dalí had written the sentence *Parfois je crache par plaisir sur le portrait de ma mère*. "Sometimes I spit for pleasure on my mother's portrait".

When the news of this startling act reached the Dalí family's home in Figueres, the consternation was absolute. Anna Maria Dalí recalled it this way in her memoirs:

"Salvador had returned from Paris. His face had an expression of exalted rancour. My father allowed him to go to Cadaqués with Luis Buñuel, believing that after a period of rest Salvador would find himself again ... and we were beginning to think that for the coming Christmas he would be the same person he always had been, for we could not even remotely imagine what Salvador had done during his last stay in Paris, which had gone beyond all limits. We found out about it in an article by Eugeni d'Ors published in *La Gaceta Literaria* in Madrid: Salvador had publicly reneged on the fundamental basis of his life.

"When we learned about it, my father refused to allow Salvador into the house. He could leave our home immediately, since all he felt for everything that was ours was such immense hatred.

"An absolute, dreadful silence came over our house. It was as if Salvador had died, or as if he had killed all of us. It destroyed our home, I think for ever more."

The evidence of the crime, the canvas on which Salvador Dalí's disordered mind splattered the memory that has remained of him, wanting to splatter that of his mother, now belongs to the Musée National d'Art Moderne of the Centre Georges Pompidou in Paris.

CHAPTER 7

The veil of Isis

The oil painting *Le jeu lugubre* (*The Lugubrious Game*), which Dalí produced shortly after meeting Gala, was bought by the peculiar Viscount de Noailles, as the artist himself wrote in his book *The Secret Life of Salvador Dalí*.

Anyone unversed in Dalinian lore who has seen a reproduction of the painting will have thought immediately that its title corresponds very little, if at all, to the impression it makes, which is one of discomfort and a certain disgust. But this hardly matters, because the titles of the Surrealists, and particularly Dalí's, are chosen entirely at random. Since this is not an abstract picture but a kind of cigarette card with human (if dehumanised) figures, and with portions of human bodies scattered in space, we feel compelled to ask what on earth it claims to represent. In a corner in the foreground there is a boy with excrement-stained pants embracing a doll – or is it a human figure? – who is covering his ace as if in shame while holding in his hand a melting, pasty substance.

What on earth is this all about? The incredible Dalí wrote, in the *Secret Life*: "My painting *Le jeu lugubre* was beginning to worry my friends. The excrement-stained pants were painted with such loving realism that everyone wondered if I was a coprophagist. The possibility that I suffered from this repugnant disease had caused them true concern, and it was Gala who decided to talk to me about it, and she said: '*If you want to use these images to proselytise in favour of a vice you consider proper to a genius, it has the risk of weakening your work, of reducing it to a psychopathological document.*' Gala's tone and tense expression forced me to tell the truth: 'I swear to you that I'm not a coprophagist. I feel the same horror that you do for this kind of deviation. But I consider the scatological elements as terrorising elements, as I do blood.'"

André Thirion, a veteran French Surrealist who knew Dalí, without making any allusion to coprophagy, has explained in a different manner the supposed significance of the picture of the boy with the messy pants, uncovering intimate details of the dominant psychology among the Parisian Surrealists:

"*The Lugubrious Game* relates, in particular, the battle fought by Dalí against his father, represented in the works of 1930 with the excellent features of *The Great Masturbator* or *William Tell.* Dalí pretended that, when he painted *The Lugubrious Game,* he was still afraid of his father's mental voracity, an active malice that would have prevented him from remaining with Gala, which put an end, at least for a time, to the masturbations in front of the mirror that were then Dalí's sex life.

"His revolt against the family was violent at that time; it had social dimensions, as is proved by *Un chien andalou,* a film which is very anarchistic, an aspect that would be radicalised by the Surrealist group, who increased its rage. Dalí submitted totally to the ideology of the Surrealist group, in which the family was detested. Some members of the group, if they talked about their mother, would merely call her *salope* ['bitch' or 'slut']. But there were a lot of contradictions. Breton spoke very badly of his mother and father, but they came to visit him in Paris at least once a year, and during that time we never saw him. Éluard regularly went to visit his mother, who often sent him large sums of money. Tanguy used to go to Brittany to visit his family. Sadoul and I spent our holidays with the family in Loraine. Aragon often saw his mother, who lived in Neuilly. And yet we always had an insult on our lips, ready for the irreparable. The inscription Dalí wrote on one of his works, *Je crache sur le portrait de ma mère*, was received very favourably by the Surrealist group. It demonstrated that Dalí held back for nothing. With the pretext of the inscription, his father kicked him out of the house. It was the last straw. His father didn't like any of his ideas. All traditions were trampled on, and when Dalí threw himself into the arms of a foreign woman who was older than him, married, with a child, and penniless, that was the end. Dalí's father saw Gala as a whore, with the appetites of a praying mantis."

André Thirion was not exaggerating when he described the attitudes of Breton's clan to the figure of the mother. There is documentary proof of it in a little work published in 1925 by Paul Éluard and Benjamin Péret: *152 proverbes mis au goût du jour* (*152 proverbs adapted to today's tastes*), a collection of nonsense mixed with the occasional peculiar proclamation, such as '*You have to hit your mother while she's still young.*'

Paris, 1930. Some of the Paris Surrealists. Top, left to right: Paul Éluard, Hans Arp, Yves Tanguy and René Crevel. Bottom: Tristan Tzara, André Breton, Salvador Dalí, Max Ernst and Man Ray. (A)

The idle Parisian bourgeois youths who gathered around the banner of Surrealism were trying to attract the attention of adult society in any way they could. They achieved it when the famous writer Paul Claudel, who was approaching 60, lost his temper and, forgetting for a moment his cultured, elegant style of his prose, fired at them an insult which in those days still had its force: *pédérastes*!

But the brazenness of the Surrealists cannot be explained merely by the irresponsibility and amorality of young bourgeois rebels. Other elements are involved.

In a personal notebook from her adolescent years, Gala had written that she considered herself "hysterical, depraved, with the instincts of a whore." And Dalí – although his word must not be taken without precaution – once said that Gala had suffered from mental disorders in her youth.

Max Ernst suffered from anxiety attacks.

Joan Miró had had hallucinations while living in Paris.

Yves Tanguy brought on hallucinations artificially.

Luis Buñuel, according to Professor Romà Gubern, had "the soul of an erotomaniac" and was haunted for the rest of his life by the frustration of never having dared to make a pornographic film.

André Masson, who split from the Surrealists in 1943, spent some time in a psychiatric hospital.

Francis Picabia had also been interned in psychiatric centres more than once.

Antonin Artaud, who joined the Surrealist group in 1924, was often shut up in mental asylums, including an entire decade at the end of his life.

Éluard, apparently a peaceful man, had written, shortly after his separation from Gala, *J'ai beaucoup d'envie de me tuer*, "I feel a strong urge to kill myself."

Suicide, in particular, was an obsessive idea among the Surrealists. The French writer Maurice Nadeau, an admirer and historian of Breton's group, said that "What most surprised the readers of the first issue of the magazine *Révolution Surréaliste* was the publication of a systematic set of statistics, from a specific period, of cases of suicide collected from the newspapers and transcribed in the magazine, with no comment whatsoever but including a photograph of Germaine Berton, a woman who had just murdered a man, surrounded by all of the Surrealists and certain figures they admired, such as Sigmund Freud, Chirico or Picasso."

The editors of the magazine continued the theme in issue number 2, asking readers to reply to a survey on the question *Is suicide a solution?* One letter received in answer to the question was signed by a certain E. Gengenbach, who said he had been expelled from the clergy for having had a relationship with an actress, and that he had thought of killing himself but had finally changed his mind.

But other readers of the magazine, sympathisers or members of the Surrealist group, met a bad end. A certain Jacques Rigaut had written a piece he entitled *Papiers posthumes,* in which he said "I am on the side of death," and had then killed himself.

Cinéma Studio 28, Paris, after the destruction caused by a group of vandals in protest against the showing of *L'âge d'or,* the second film made by Buñuel and Dalí, in 1930. (A)

The Dadaist Jacques Vaché, a colleague of Apollinaire, had taken his life after repeatedly performing acts of madness.

René Crevel committed suicide in 1935. And in his *Secret Life*, Dalí wrote "Crevel was the third Surrealist who killed himself, thus corroborating the survey made by the movement in its beginnings."

Robert Desnos died during the Second World War, but in the 1930's, practising hypnotism with the Surrealist group, he described in detail his colleagues' dreams of violent death.

The maniacal temptation to take one's own life did not only pursue the Surrealists of Paris. The Georgian poet Vladimir Mayakovsky, the leading figure of the Soviet Futurists, killed himself in Moscow in 1930. And the Romanian magistrate Demetresco, who wrote very strange stories under the pseudonym of Urmuz and is considered the precursor of Surrealism in his home country, committed suicide in a public park in 1923, at the age of 40. His compatriot Eugen Ionescu (Eugène Ionesco), the propagator of the 'Theatre of the Absurd,' spoke out for him in 1965: "Urmuz is one of the precursors of the universal literary revolt, one of the prophets of the dislocation of social forms, of the thought and language of this world which is today falling apart before our eyes, a world as absurd as Urmuz's heroes."

Far removed from such apologies and the exercises of intellectual justification, the French writer and anthropologist Michel Leiris, who as a young poet had been associated with Breton's group, wrote in his autobiographical work *L'âge d'homme* (*Manhood*), published in 1939, a harrowing confession, more revealing than any other such text, of the pathological fits of delirium he suffered, similar to those experienced by other young men drawn to the Surrealist movement:

"At that time I spent most of my nights in Montmartre, going from one *boîte* to another. Alcohol, smoke, music and people made up the mental stimulant we considered most suitable for favouring inspiration.

"One day, early in July 1925, when leaving a literary banquet, I was mistreated by the police and almost lynched for having cried out against them and the public. To tell the truth, I had doped myself beforehand with two or three aperitifs, because I wanted to make a scene but was not sure I would have the courage.

"I had to stay in bed for a week after the beating-up they gave me, but my obsession would not cease. I turned words around, seeking deep significance in them. I wrote down my dreams to extract the secret from them. Once I dreamed I had swallowed a poison that was going to kill me. I woke up screaming...

"The relationship with a strange figure who had recently joined our group, an expelled seminarist, a mythomaniac turned adventurer [the supposed ex-clergyman Gengenbach] caused me to lose my equilibrium entirely. I had always longed to dissolve myself in a kind of voluntary madness, like Gérard de Nerval, and suddenly I felt possessed by an acute fear of really going mad. A punishment for my inhuman temptations to lose my reason and for having wanted to invade the mystery by raising the veil of Isis.

"One night I felt such an attack of anxiety and panic that I asked my mother to let me sleep with her..."

In this way, Leiris returned to the maternal lair.

Dalí, having reneged on his dead mother and been expelled from the paternal home, saw himself condemned to continue his erratic journey into the depths of the night.

PART THREE

CHAPTER 8

The discovery of America

New York, 1934-35

In the year 1626, the leaders of the Manhattan tribe must have felt they had made a killing by selling their island to the Dutchman Peter Minuit for some 20 dollars' worth of trinkets. In 1931, it was the New York art dealer Julien Levy who believed he had made a historic deal by buying for just 250 dollars a small oil painting (24 × 33 cm) signed by Salvador Dalí. In the background, a desolate seascape; in the foreground, three pocket watches apparently made of some soft material, draped over a tree branch, a shell, a box, as if drying out in the sun. To some people they may look like fried eggs; to others, banana skins. In any case, the title, *The Persistence of Memory*, clears up the mystery a little: Dalí continually recalls the landscape of the Cadaqués of his youth, he cannot get it out of his head, and it becomes the backdrop for his anxieties.

Thanks to a number of dealers, Dalí's works were beginning to make inroads into artistic circles of the East Coast of the US, where innovative products imported from Europe, particularly from Paris, were arousing the interest of certain multimillionaire snobs. This interest was heightened in artistic fields by the wealthy classes' lack of conviction concerning the culture of the United States itself.

After the First World War, the nine million-plus square kilometres of the US contained some 120 museums, approximately the same number as the Principality of Catalonia has in an area three hundred times smaller.

The refined Impressionistic and symbolist painting of James Whistler, from Massachusetts, was better known and more admired in London and Paris than in his homeland. The extraordinary Impressionist-styled watercolour artist and oil portraitist John Singer Sargent, born in Italy of American parents, was certainly commissioned to paint the murals of the Boston Public Library and the Widener Library in Harvard, but only after having his work admired in London, Paris and Rome. The Boston-born landscape artist Winslow Homer, one of the leading painters of the Civil War, was appreciated in his own time thanks to the reproductions made of his inimitable watercolours. But by the 1930's, all of these artists were ignored or despised by rich, ignorant New Yorkers who had taken an interest in the art world and who apparently went into ecstasy over Duchamp's urinal.

The American sociologist Alvin Toffler, a fervent defender of the Stars and Stripes, was still complaining in the 1960's of the "inferiority complex the United States suffers with regard to its own culture."

In Great Britain, however, as was to be expected, the atmosphere was different. Dalí's first individual exhibition at a London gallery, in 1934, met with a very negative reception. The works included drawings of tortures and bloody sexual perversions that illustrated the *Chants de Maldoror* by the self-styled Count of Lautréamont, the mysterious and half-demented follower of Sade. "This is utter rubbish, addressed, I suppose, to those who consider themselves very clever and modern," wrote Clive Bell of the *New Statesman*, for whom one glance at the exhibition was enough to issue the definitive verdict.

But Dalí was like a rampant stallion, and after his victorious campaign in Paris, his goal was to conquer New York. Thanks to the Parisian dealers' contacts with the families of Wall Street financiers, Dalí had managed to exhibit in the Big Apple, sell his works by the barrowload and make himself heard in French and Catalan to audiences of journalists who only understood the language of Clark Gable and Fred Astaire.

Among the New York fans of Dalí and Gala – who by now accompanied him everywhere – there was Caresse, the wife of Harry Crosby, a less-than-overworked young member of the family that owned the Morgan Bank, which had monopolised the finances of Wall Street. And when, after four months of frenzied activity in New York, the Dalís were preparing to return to Europe, Caresse Crosby and Julien Levy's wife had the idea of organising a fancy dress ball as a farewell gesture. The champagne would be French, *naturellement*; extravagance would be *de rigueur*; and fun was ensured.

Gala arrived wearing in a costume that froze the party-goers in their tracks. Meryle Secrest, the former *Washington Post* journalist who had turned to writing biographies of artists, including Dalí, described the scene as follows:

"Everyone agrees that the object Gala was exhibiting on her head, in the middle of an enormous black hat, was a doll that imitated the dead body of a baby. The doll had a wound on its forehead, carefully painted there by Dalí. The wound was teeming with ants, and a lobster was gripping its skull with its pincers. A pair of gloves, stretched out on either side like wings, completed this macabre imagery."

The reporters demanded, where had the Dalís got such a strange and horrendous idea from? Wasn't that dead body a direct allusion to the kidnapping and murder in 1932 of the 21-month-old son of America's hero Charles Lindbergh, the first aviator to fly non-stop from New York to Paris?

Everyone had read about the case. On 19 September 1934, just a few weeks before the Dalís arrived in New York, huge newspaper headlines announced that the petty burglar Bruno Richard Hauptmann had been arrested for the horrific crime committed in March 1932.

An American publication reproduced this photograph of Gala in her costume with a wounded doll in her hat, alluding to Charles Lindbergh's murdered son. The title of the accompanying text is explicit: MADNESS. (AA)

"The particularly revolting details of the event were still fresh in people's minds," Secrest wrote, "but were the Dalís capable of using the case with this kind of brutal symbolism? It is something that seemed entirely believable to those who, like the French painter Henri Matisse, had heard Gala and Dalí make cynical comments along the lines of '*Take those Americans for all they're worth!*'"

Recalling that exploit of Dalí and Gala in his memoirs, Luis Buñuel wrote, "It was something that the Americans took very badly. For them, Lindbergh was an almost sacred figure, and this was a story that could not be touched on any pretext. And Dalí, seriously admonished by his dealer, recanted before the press."

At the time, the Catalans in general knew nothing of Dalí's deeds in New York. But in Sarrià, in Barcelona, one person was following his steps closely and admiringly: J.V.

Foix, a writer who was captivated by Futurism. Curiously, Foix was a smartly-dressed middle-aged member of a distinguished family who owned one of the city's finest pastry shops. In 1935, he declared in an elitist Catalan publication that what Dalí had brought the Americans was "disturbance", and that in the same way that "Miró offered them an aesthetic, Dalí offered them a mysticism, a morality."

That Dalí's works were disturbing, no-one would place in doubt. But to say that they bore a "mysticism" shows that the learned Mr. Foix was merely tossing words around, or that he was ignorant of the exact scope of the term "mysticism". And what is more, to say that Dalí, a paradigm of an amoral human being, offered "a morality" is not merely a misconception, an incoherence; it is simply laughable, which was probably the last thing the always upright and no doubt highly-educated Mr. Foix intended. But such was the world of Dalí and his few admirers.

Once the macabre party in New York was over, the Dalís hurriedly returned to Europe. Of the dollars they had made and that Gala administered, and of how they had made them, they would not have to give explanations to anyone. But some of the ideas Dalí had expressed in public, and the attitude he had shown as a representative of Surrealism, he would be forced to explain to a kind of Sanhedrin presided over by André Breton.

In Paris they were already waiting for him.

CHAPTER 9

"Épater les bourgeois"

Paris, 1935-36

At the beginning, Breton's group, more inclined towards literature than the other arts, were considered by decent folk to be a gang of good-for-nothings who met up to have a laugh and *épater les bourgeois*. Paul Éluard himself had once confessed, "People say we write for snobs." A similar idea had developed about the artists who formed part of the group.

It is true that there was something else. According to Maurice Nadeau, "the founders of Surrealism did not believe this movement was like a new artistic school, but a way of discovering new regions which had not been explored until then: the subconscious, the marvellous, dreams, madness, states of hallucination. If to this we add everything fantastic and surprising there is in the world, we see that Surrealism is the contrary of logical conception."

There is something tragicomic in the evolution of the sectarian group of Parisian Surrealists, which progressively devoured its own members. With the growing scandal they were seeking and, indeed, creating in Parisian intelligentsia, Breton became more and more arrogant and began to see himself as the guardian of Surrealist orthodoxy, the grand inquisitor, the commissar in chief of the movement.

"When Dalí returned to Paris," Buñuel wrote in his memoirs, "and after denying to the reporters of the newspaper *Le Petit Parisien* that Gala's costume at the new York ball had anything to do with the Lindbergh case, the Surrealists called him to judgment. His offence was serious: having reneged in public on a Surrealist act! André Breton himself told me that at that moment Dalí fell on his knees and, with his eyes full of tears and hands clasped together, swore that the reporters had lied, that he had always said *yes*, it really was an allusion to Lindbergh's child."

It is plain that Dalí's word did not mean much, and in any case, the Surrealists' concern about the consequences of the amoral manipulation of the Lindbergh case was soon to be superseded by another fact: the ambivalent obsession Dalí showed towards Adolf Hitler.

The old Surrealist André Thirion offered this version: "Dalí had a quite reasonable sort of delirium in assimilating Hitler with evil, considering him a destructive genius, a modern incarnation of Maldoror. And he thought: Why not subject Hitler to the paranoico-critical method? Breton wanted to expel Dalí from the Surrealist group, considering him "guilty of counter-revolutionary acts tending to glorify Hitlerian Fascism." The meeting turned into a farce, a ceremony of confusion, because the accusers did not have a clear idea of what Hitlerism was, and they were not astute enough to maintain a controversy with Dalí … In any case, Éluard persuaded Dalí to relinquish introducing Hitler into the paranoico-critical method … To clarify matters, Dalí gave a couple of violently anti-Hitler speeches in Barcelona and informed his Parisian friends about them."

Deutschland, erwache! Germany, awake! Hitler cried from the huge platform in the main square of Munich. *Sieg Heil!* Hail Victory! was the thunderous reply of the electrified masses, right arms outstretched in the salute the Nazis had borrowed from the Italian Fascists and they in turn from the Roman legions.

The German eagle was still licking its wounds from the humiliating defeat in the First World War in 1918, but was now flexing its wings again, threatening the unstable European peace and aggravating the ferocious social conflicts within individual countries, where Fascists and Stalinists were clearing the way for the Nazis on the one hand and the Soviet commissars on the other.

The majority of the Surrealists of Paris appear in this photographic montage, published in number 12 of the *Révolution Surréaliste* in December 1929. Dalí is the second down in the left-hand column. (AA)

Obviously the Surrealists had no influence in international politics, but Breton's group were decided allies of the Soviets, and some of the members had acted prematurely as *agents provocateurs*, with that kind of ambivalent provocations that were also perpetrated by the Fascistoid Futurists, the early Nazis and the Iberian anarchists.

In 1923, the anarchist poet Louis Aragon, an admirer of Apollinaire, had proclaimed, "Our heroes are Violette Nozière, the parricide, the anonymous criminal of common law, conscious and refined sacrilege!"

In 1927, Breton had written in the *Second Manifesto of Surrealism*, "The simplest Surrealist act consists in picking up the pistols and firing them into the crowd at random," precisely an act which Jacques Vaché, Apollinaire's insane colleague, had threatened to commit.

Buñuel and Dalí were almost certainly incapable of picking up a gun without their hands trembling. On the other hand, in 1930 they were capable of filming *L'âge d'or*, which begins with a view of menacing scorpions, a band of armed roughs and skeletons of priests rotting in the sun, and finishes with the protagonist throwing a bishop through a window. This provocation received the appropriate and predictable responses: the newspaper *L'Humanité*, the mouthpiece of the French Communist Party, gave it high praise, and the young lions of the Ligue Patriotique attacked the Parisian cinema where the film was showing. In Madrid, the response was truly 'surrealistic', to use the term in the vulgar, generalised sense it now has: something absurd that makes us laugh. Dalí's admirer Ernesto Giménez Caballero, the publisher of *La Gaceta Literaria*, suggested that those who had attacked the Paris cinema should join forces with the Surrealists, to make revolutionary violence complete!

After 1930, Aragon, now living with Elsa Triolet, Mayakovsky's sister-in-law, explained the growing politicisation of the Surrealists in stodgy, opaque Stalinist prose: "The recognition of dialectical materialism as the sole revolutionary philosophy and its acceptance by intellectuals proceeding from idealism constitute the essential features of the evolution of the Surrealists. This evolution implies the acceptance of the action of the Third International as the sole revolutionary action and implies the necessity of giving support to the action in France of the French Communist Party, the French section of this International."

But at the end of 1935, Breton, Éluard and Crevel were expelled from the Communist Party, while Aragon, preferring to further his career with the Stalinists, abandoned the Surrealists.

For his part, Pierre Drieu La Rochelle, who had made himself a name in the avant-garde, took another route, which always obsessed Aragon, Jean-Paul Sartre and other writers of their ilk. Drieu La Rochelle, a supporter of socialism, had positive traits as a writer. At the age of 28, along with Aragon, Tristan Tzara, Benjamin Péret and other Dadaists and future Surrealists, he had taken part in a bizarre act presented as a trial against the traditionalist writer Maurice Barrès. But Drieu La Rochelle turned towards Fascist socialism, of which he was a brilliant propagandist, and would eventually come to work openly for the collaborative Vichy government during the Nazi occupation of France.

Dalí, for the moment, remained at Breton's side, but the Parisian Surrealist sect was beginning to severely restrict his ego.

Hitler? Now *there* was a good theme for a Dalinian painting! At first, following Éluard's advice, Dalí abstained from producing any work directly referring to the German dictator. But he did not forget the idea, and three or four years later he decided to use it.

The Enigma of Hitler is the title of a canvas that Dalí painted some time in the late 1930's, now contained in the Queen Sofía National Art Centre Museum in Madrid. Any viewer wanting to know which in which political direction, if any, Dalí was leaning at that moment will be

The Enigma of Hitler. Oil on canvas. 51 × 79 cm.

disappointed and frustrated. The composition, which is as masterly as the brush strokes, consists basically of two elements appearing in the foreground: a black telephone with the cord cut, hanging from a branch of a pruned bush, hovers over a bowl of soup, on the surface of which floats a passport-style photo of Hitler. From the same branch there also hangs an umbrella, which presumably represents the one always carried by Neville Chamberlain, the British Prime Minister who met Hitler a number of times to attempt to block his demands, but who after the betrayal of the Munich Agreement was forced to declare war on Nazi Germany in 1939. The picture, then, would appear to have been painted in 1939, the cut phone cord symbolising the breakdown of talks between Chamberlain and Hitler and the start of World War Two. According to this interpretation, Dalí merely limited himself to recording a fact, without tilting the ideological balance one way or the other.

From the strictly artistic point of view, *The Enigma of Hitler* is one of Dalí's finest works: one of the cleanest, most balanced and most free of paranoid elements. The scene is portrayed against the inevitable backdrop of the cloudy sky and the rocks of the coast of Cadaqués, more imagined than realistically portrayed, but the contrast between the sharply-drawn foreground elements and the hazy background is excellent. It is easy to see in the composition the influence of the hard close-ups used in the cinema. The work can also be considered a precursor of the cover illustrations of modern magazines and advertisements, in which the use of the extreme close-up has become a hackneyed stereotype.

Dalí's geographical and biographical itinerary in the late 1930's and early 1940's was extraordinarily eventful. Having settled in Paris in 1935, he made brief visits to London and Catalonia (where it seems he had a fleeting reunion with his father), and then, invited by Edward James, one of his patrons, he went to Ravello, on the Italian Mediterranean coast opposite Capri, a place then frequented by foreign millionaires taking their summer holidays and by the top brass of the then triumphant Italian Fascist movement.

Dalí spent the first half of 1936 with one foot in Paris and the other in the house he was having built in Port-lligat, a small bay just outside Cadaqués. The social and political situation, both in France and particularly in Catalonia and Spain as a whole, was red-hot. Nevertheless, a collective Surrealist exhibition had opened in Paris, and to mark the occasion Dalí published in a French magazine a chaotic article which more or less said that the Nazi swastika symbolised the amalgamation of the right and the left – an idea which clearly could give no satisfaction to one side nor the other.

A few weeks later another collective Surrealist exhibition opened in London, with a more international character – and was boycotted by both Fascists and Stalinists.

In contrast, a private London gallery opened its doors wide to Dalí, and despite lacerating reviews in the serious newspapers and magazines, it seems that some fifteen works were sold immediately. In their luxurious London hotel room, Gala and Dalí raised their champagne glasses to celebrate the successful outcome of the deal. On the other side of the room, the radio began to announce the latest news ... and the Dalís quickly began to pack.

CHAPTER 10

War

Europe, 1936 – USA, 1940

18 July 1936. The latest news on the radio: "General Franco, the military commander of the Canary Islands, has rebelled against the Republican government in Madrid and disembarked in the south of the Iberian Peninsula at the head of the colonial troops from Morocco. In many Spanish cities the military garrisons have taken to the streets in support of the revolt."

With the help of German and Italian volunteer pilots, the horde of brutal colonial troops, both Moroccans and mercenaries of the Spanish Foreign Legion, were flying through the clouds over the Strait of Gibraltar and disembarking in Andalusia, prepared to fight all the way to the Pyrenees, in what was the first and largest airlift of troops in history.

Franco's rebels enjoyed the complicity of a large number of the regiments quartered in the Peninsula and the sympathies of certain sections of the civilian population.

In Barcelona, the troops who had rebelled, with the assistance of a number of civilians, were immediately defeated by the police and the workers' militias. But the legitimate autonomous government of Catalonia became a hostage of the militias, whose actions degenerated into pillaging and indiscriminate killing. An unimaginable witch-hunt of Catalan civilians broke out within the Republican camp.

In Granada, in the heart of rural Andalusia, Franco's uprising triumphed in a matter of hours, and one of its first acts was the execution by firing squad of a poet: García Lorca.

What effect must the news of these events have had in the soul of Salvador Dalí? Did he think of the uncertain situation of his family in Figueres or Cadaqués, as he was returning to Paris with Gala? Or did he only think that his house in Portlligat would be occupied?

Whatever he was thinking, in any case Dalí had, or could have had, an insuperable informer and to some extent protector in Barcelona, in the person of his close friend from childhood Met Miravitlles, his collaborator on the film *Un chien andalou*, now the secretary of the feared Committee of Anti-Fascist Militias. The Militias, which must have struck fear into people like the liberal-republican notary Mr. Dalí Cusí – suddenly considered by the anarchists

General view of the destruction of Gernika. (BN)

as one more bourgeois to be struck down – dominated the situation in Catalonia. They must have struck even more fear into J.V. Foix, not just because he always wore a suit and tie and bowler hat but because of the pastry shop his family owned. More than one compatriot had been shot in the back of the neck and dumped into the gutter in those days simply because he wore a tie and hat, whether he was a true reactionary bourgeois or merely a modest shop assistant or a badly-paid factory clerk.

The principal prey of the anarchists' inspection patrols, who were euphemistically termed 'uncontrolled', were the nuns and priests. The peaceful rector of the parish of St Peter in Dalí's home town of Figueres, Reverend Pere Aolas i Vergés, was assassinated on 8 September of that fateful year of 1936.

But the Spanish Civil War, with its beastly massacres on both sides, would not prevent the Dalís from pursuing their lucrative career. In the early autumn of 1936 the couple visited Florence and Cortina d'Ampezzo. In November they were in Paris, and in December back in New York, where the artist would draw the attention of *Time* magazine, the second largest in circulation after *Reader's Digest.*

The chief editor of *Time* at that moment was not the most brilliant the magazine has had in its long history. Moreover, as *Reader's Digest* played the card of the traditional tastes of the 'average' Americans of the Midwest, *Time*'s strategy was to appeal to cosmopolitan types, particularly on the eastern seaboard, who needed to consume the latest pseudo-artistic European fashions to achieve status. Consequently, on 14 December 1936 *Time* dedicated its cover to Dalí. This would prove to be an excellent calling card on the other side of the country, in Hollywood, California, where in January 1937 Dalí had himself photographed with one of the few characters with whom he could have communicated: Harpo Marx.

The society columns of the newspapers record the Dalís' return to Europe and their passage through idyllic tourist spots in Austria, Hungary and Mussolini's Italy in March 1937, before settling once again in Paris.

That spring, the 1937 Universal Exposition of Paris opened on the esplanade of the Trocadéro, beside the Seine. Two colossal constructions of iron and concrete had been erected at the entrance. One was the pavilion representing the Soviet Union, crowned by the statue of a muscular *tovarich* brandishing the hammer and sickle. The other building, even taller, was the German pavilion, topped by a black eagle whose claws rested on the swastika. Smiling faces paraded through the Paris Exhibition while, on 26 April, aircraft of the German Condor legion at the service of Franco devastated the emblematic Basque town of Gernika, and on 29 May, while Russian planes at the service of the Republic bombarded the German warship *Deutschland* in the bay of Eivissa (Ibiza). The Basque Country (Euskadi), the Catalan countries and the provinces of Spain became the firing ranges of the USSR and the Third Reich, the training grounds for a far greater and more destructive carnage.

The fear of a new European war was causing great anxiety in France, where innumerable monuments recalled those *morts pour la patrie* in the 1914-18 bloodbath. But people had to live, and to live for the moment, and the Parisian art season, which lasted from April to July, displayed the jewels of high-quality painting in various galleries where the Surrealists were barred.

Outside the season, in January 1938 the Surrealists managed to stage an exhibition at the Paris gallery of a certain Wildenstein, suitably decorated with erotic artefacts and the usual provocations of good taste. But a ring of fire and steel was gradually encircling and choking the privileged enclaves of high society that found their entertainment in the carnival of Surrealism. From now on it would be more and more difficult to find a spa where the cannons could not be heard.

In March 1938, German troops invaded Austria. Shortly afterwards, the Condor Legion bombarded Barcelona. On

87

1 October the Nazis invaded the Sudetenland, a region of over three million German speakers in Czechoslovakian territory. But just outside Monte Carlo, on the Côte d'Azur, the queen of fashion and perfume Coco Chanel possessed a mansion that was protected from such ill winds, where she invited her *interesting* acquaintances to smoke opium – and that is where Dalí and Gala headed at the end of 1938.

Further west along the Mediterranean coast, the situation was not so safe. And on the other side of the Pyrenees, in Dalí's homeland of the Empordà, people were going hungry. A journalist from the French magazine *L'Illustration*, a special envoy in the Catalan sector of the Franco-Spanish frontier, had been witness to this. Groups of women from Figueres, some with small children, loaded like mules with sacks of vegetables on their backs, walked, at night, the thirty kilometres along the railway tracks to the village of Cervera on the other side of the border, where they exchanged their vegetables for bread and, with the permission of the frontier police, returned to Figueres with their sacks full.

But the Catalan civilian population was gripped by fear as much as by hunger. Many tip-offs from hateful or jealous neighbours led families into the blackest poverty or some of their members to interrogation centres, to torture.

Meryle Secrest, Dalí's American biographer, on the basis of statements by members of the artist's family, has said that his sister Anna Maria was detained and tortured by henchmen of the Stalinist political police, named in true Orwellian fashion the 'Military Information Service.'

Isabel Bassols, the widow of the well-known Catalan publisher and novelist Mario Lacruz, hails from Figueres and lived there alongside Anna Maria Dalí throughout the Civil War. She says, "Yes, Anna Maria was arrested and shut in prison. I don't think it can strictly be said she was tortured. She was shut up, that's true, in a small, narrow space, which caused her an obsessive anxiety, a claustrophobia that almost drove her mad. She was shut up with another young woman, the companion of the painter Josep Maria Prim i Guytó. Anna Maria was hysterical, she screamed day and night, and after a time she was released along with her cellmate. But she was disturbed and ill for a good nine months. The reason, or pretext, for the arrest was that they had supposedly been with Josep Maria Prim on board a friend's yacht when it was intercepted by the Stalinist police. According to the police, they found a diary with names and annotations that indicated espionage for the *nationals* [Francoists]."

Another document relating this episode is a letter Dalí wrote to Buñuel, conserved in the Luis Buñuel Archive in Madrid: "The *reds* shut my sister in prison, in Barcelona, for twenty days, and martyrised her. She's gone mad. Now she's in Cadaqués. They have to force-feed her and she shits in the bed. Imagine the tragedy of my father, who's been robbed of *everything*, and who has to live in a room in a boarding-house in Figueres. Naturally I'm sending dollars to him..."

Secrest says, "Anna Maria always believed, on the basis of we don't know what testimonies, that it was Gala and Dalí who had reported her." On the face of it, this suspicion seems difficult to believe due to the circumstances of the moment. Gala and Dalí never set foot in Catalonia during the Civil War, and reports to the police in those days were not made by telephone nor by telegram. Anna Maria's belief must, rather, have been based on the idea that Gala wished her all the harm possible, and this certainly is corroborated by all of the witnesses of the time. And at the same time, Anna Maria felt an instinctive repulsion, as did her father, towards Gala, and it could also be that, added to this repulsion, there was the hatred aroused by the diabolical woman from the steppes who had robbed her of the love of her adored brother Salvador.

In January 1939 Barcelona was occupied by Franco's troops. In February the Republican troops, retreating towards the French frontier, left two indelible memories in

Ruins of the village of Llers after being dynamited by retreating Republican troops in the last days of the Spanish Civil War. (AL)

the Empordà: in Figueres, already devastated by Francoist bombardments, they dynamited the castle; and in Llers, the cradle of the Dalí lineage, they blew up the church and the old part of the village.

In the final weeks of the Civil War, even though the exhausted population of Catalonia was simply longing for the end of the conflict, whoever was the victor, no-one could be sure of what would be the intentions and actions of the Francoist *liberators* towards the Catalan civilians. In Cadaqués they had the privilege of finding out immediately. Carles Rahola i Llorens, a historian and writer from a well-to-do local family, a Catalanist and a republican but not a member of any political party, was executed by firing squad on 15 March.

Nevertheless, there had been so much suffering that for many people the end of the war meant a profound, if short-lived, relief. In his letter to Buñuel, Dalí finished by saying: "My father has turned into a fanatical devotee of Franco, according to what he tells me in his delirious letters ... The attempt at revolution has been so disastrous

90

that people prefer Franco ... lifelong Catalanists, federal republicans, militant anticlericals, write to me declaring themselves delighted with the new regime."

As always, Dalí's word has to be taken with great precaution. But his father's change of political beliefs is borne out by the testimony of a friend of his, the prolific Empordanese writer Josep Pla – who had also sided with the *nationals* – who in 1958 wrote, with his customary cynicism:

"It is too easy to recall the contradictions, I mean the opportunism, of Mr. Dalí Cusí. But who could we not recall? It would be extremely amusing for me to describe the recalcitrant agnosticism of his long, early decades, and, even more, that unforgettable scene that took place in his vegetable garden, where he told me, gesticulating happily in front of his ostentatious broccoli and lettuces: 'These broccoli, these lettuces, friend Pla, do they not arouse in you the unquestionable existence of a first cause, of an omnipotent, eternal and universal God?' He was a permanent militant, both when he never went to mass and when he never failed to go."

In Catalonia and Spain, the survivors of the Civil War were putting their lives back together as best they could, and in the rest of Europe the probabilities of the outbreak of another international conflagration were ever more perceptible.

In the United States, President Roosevelt was attempting to convince his reticent fellow Americans that the international situation was becoming critical, and that the US, which was already supplying arms to Britain, would have no alternative but to call up its young men and send them into the war, as it had done with their fathers' generation. But in New York preparations were going ahead for a Universal Exposition or World's Fair, and in the spring of 1939 its directors had commissioned Dalí to put on an 'entertaining' show for a section of the exhibition, following his tremendous publicity *coups*: the successful exhibition of paintings at Julien Levy's gallery, the scandalous stunt at the Bonwit-Teller store, and *Life* magazine's description of him as "one of the richest young painters in the world."

After their spring stay in New York, the Dalís returned to Europe planning to rest. But however much they might have wanted to place themselves above the fray, they would soon find themselves forced to run like all the other earthly mortals.

After Hitler's invasion of Poland in September 1939, Britain and France declared war on Germany. Those who could do so fled from Paris, and Gala and Dalí rented a house on the beach at Arcachon, near Bordeaux, where some fugitive acquaintances of theirs had already settled. But when, on 14 June 1940, the Nazis marched into Paris and flew the swastika banner from the Eiffel Tower, the Dalís realised that the only way for them to escape from the war was to cross the Atlantic.

Gala rushed to Lisbon to carry out the formalities for sailing to the United States. Dalí made a fleeting visit to Catalonia, where he met his father and went to Portlligat, only to see his house half demolished, with doors hanging off their hinges, with no furniture, no crockery, with the wind howling through the shattered window panes.

With a permit from the Francoist authorities, Dalí was able to cross Spanish territory and meet up in Madrid with his two old Spanish comrades, Eugenio Montes and Ernesto Giménez Caballero, now both elevated to the highest ranks of the Falange, the Spanish Fascist party. Despite these good connections, Franco's government refused Dalí permission to leave the country and enter Portugal. Being informed of this, Alfred Barr, the director of the New York Museum of Modern Art, who had already pressurised the American ambassador in Paris, announced his opinion that even if Dalí was politically a Catalan patriot and a radical, he was first and foremost an artist. It seems that the young Nelson Rockefeller, of the family that controlled the powerful Standard Oil Company, was able to bring influence to bear on the US government to intervene in the matter. Be that as it may, the fact is that in a few days Dalí obtained the necessary permits to leave Franco's Spain safe and sound and rejoin Gala in Lisbon, where they immediately set sail for New York, arriving on 16 August 1940.

The welcome the artist received in the Big Apple caused confusion and controversy among the museum managers, art critics and press. While Mr. Barr of the MOMA, who was clearly not the best informed of people, said that Dalí was "a radical", which to most Americans means an extreme left-wing revolutionary, Emily Genauer, the art columnist of the New York World-Telegram, believed that Dalí's imagery was in fact "Fascistic".

Amid the controversies, Dalí, shrewder than some of his critics and certainly less honest, prepared to officiate over the ceremony of avant-garde confusion in the generous country that had opened its arms to him.

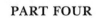

PART FOUR

CHAPTER 11

Avida Dollars

United States of America, 1940-48

"Despite the incredible theatricality of his public life, Dalí gives the impression of being entirely sincere. He is an eccentric genius. The philosophy of the Surrealists has provided him with the justification for his eccentricities and a method of using them to his own benefit. In a world where – fortunately! – most people try to behave in the most normal manner possible, Dalí simply does the opposite."

With this lucid analysis, Winthrop Sargeant, writing in *Life* magazine in September 1945, unveiled Dalí's strategy, but without going any deeper into his true personality. Sargeant's diagnosis was probably shared, under their breath, by many of the people with whom Dalí dealt (in every sense) in the States.

And yet there was no shortage of not-so-intelligent intellectuals who took seriously the artist's theoretical or ideological proclamations. And no shortage, either, of the typical businessmen from the dusty Midwest who, having made a fortune on the East Coast, believed that a few lavishly-framed paintings by some famous artist would bestow on them the class lacking in the houses of the honest ranchers back home. Unencumbered by aesthetic taste, they swallowed the Dalinian propaganda without realising that in fact it consisted of no more than advertising slogans designed to sell the 'Dalí brand'.

It was in the young homeland of Coca-Cola that the commercial skills of the crafty, crazy Catalan artist met with their greatest success. He had still not been in the US for a year and yet everything was going his way. In a hotel in Pebble Beach, California, in 1941, the prosperous European refugees from the barbarity of the War, Mr. and Mrs. Salvador Dalí, threw a Surrealist party with the grateful attendance of a number of heavyweights from the factory of dreams, including Bob Hope, Clark Gable, Bing Crosby and the sombre Alfred Hitchcock.

The surprise Japanese attack on Pearl Harbor on 7 December 1941 was the immediate cause of the United States' entry into World War Two and of the inevitable commotion in American society. But this did not prevent the New York Museum of Modern Art from keeping its doors open, and at that time it was presenting a retrospective exhibition of Dalí's paintings (and, simultaneously, another retrospective, on Miró). Apart from that, Dalí staged an exhibition at the James Levy gallery, and he was commissioned to design the sets and costumes for the operetta *Labyrinth*, presented at the New York Metropolitan Theatre.

In order to maintain the favour of his peculiar clientele and the attention of the press, Dalí could not allow himself to fall into routine: from time to time he had to make a leap without a net even more daring than the last one. So, in 1942, he published in New York the book *The Secret Life of Salvador Dalí by Salvador Dalí*, a large part of which seems to have been written in Virginia, at a house belonging to Caresse Crosby, then Dalí's principal patron and the promoter of the book, and the same woman who, seven years earlier, had been the hostess of the party in New York where Dalí and Gala played the macabre joke referring to the Lindbergh case.

The translators of the work sweated blood. Meredith Etherington-Smith, the author of a biography of Dalí published in London, has said that "The original manuscript was written in an execrable, illegible French." Caresse

Crosby had commissioned the English version from Haakon M. Chevalier, a translator of French novels, and the Spanish version from Cèsar August Jordana, a Catalan writer living in exile in Latin America who had done translations for the Government of Catalonia. Having examined the original, Jordana said "Mr. Dalí's manuscript, with regard to handwriting, spelling and syntax, is probably one of the most fantastically indecipherable documents that have ever flowed from a writer's hand. The manuscript is written on yellow paper, in almost unintelligible handwriting, almost without punctuation nor division into paragraphs, with a crazed, capricious spelling that would flood a lexicographer's brow with sweat."

Everything indicates that the first version in English and the successive translations or adaptations were, in reality, rewritings that ordered and improved the magmatic original text. But it makes no difference. The book is a true Dalinian work, and its contents justify the introductory note with which the publishers Gallimard presented the

Cover of the US edition of *The Secret Life of Salvador Dalí* (GdC)

French adaptation: "This book is a monument erected by Salvador Dalí to his own glory. If all modesty is absent from it, his sincerity is, on the other hand, overwhelming. The author strips himself of his secrets with insolent brazenness."

Dalí the morbid voyeur became here a provocative exhibitionist, just as he had always done. Now all he had to do was sit back on his sofa and wait for the critics' reactions – the more furious, the better – to complete this raving work of self-promotion.

The unbearable gossip columnist Elsa Maxwell recommended the book to anyone who wanted to take a trip through "the labyrinths of psychoneurosis." And a publicity item in *Time* said, "The question has always been, Is Dalí crazy? The book indicates that Dalí is as crazy as a goat."

The serious critics massacred the book. "The navel-contemplating author of the book is not a Buddha but a spoilt child," wrote Howard Devree in the *New York Times*. "It is like the work of a mental patient," said A. Davidson in the *Art Digest*. In the *New Republic*, M. Cowley predicted that the book could symbolise in the future the collapse of the basic values of Western Europe.

An English writer who was profoundly indignant with Dalí was the idealist George Orwell. He knew a thing or two about Catalonia, because during the Spanish Civil War he had enlisted as a volunteer with the POUM, the Catalan Trotskyist party. But at the time when *The Secret Life of Salvador Dalí* appeared, Orwell had more serious problems on his mind. His wife Eileen was dying, and Orwell could not raise the fifty pounds to pay for the operation she needed. He was then writing *Animal Farm*, his ferocious satire on Stalin, and he could not find a publisher because the dictator of all the Russias was then an ally of Britain in the struggle against the Nazis.

Eileen died. Just a few months later, on 17 August 1945, with Germany and Japan defeated and the war over, and Britain no longer needing to mollify Stalin, *Animal Farm* was finally published to tremendous and lasting success. The combative Orwell was then free to focus the sights of his pen on Dalí, and with the same marksmanship as he had shown in Stalin's case, he wrote, "Individuals like Dalí are undesirable, and a society in which they can flourish has something wrong in its bosom ... Dalí's book is a direct and unmistakeable assault on decency."

Dalí, of course, was unmoved. Meanwhile, to commissions from Helena Rubinstein, Elsa Schiaparelli and other millionaires, he had painted oil portraits of the wives of big American businessmen, which were displayed in 1943 at the Knoedler Gallery, and he had also met the wealthy Colorado tycoon Reynolds Morse and his wife Eleanor Reese, who began to buy paintings of all kinds from him.

Other relationships, though, did not fare so well. According to Meryle Secrest, Dalí painted a horrific portrait of a certain Mrs. Nichols, which she and her husband quietly paid for and immediately disposed of. Dalí found out about this and told Mrs. Nichols, "I have recovered the painting, I have bought it. Now I keep it in my workshop, I practise magic on it and stick needles into the eyes..." Years later, Mrs. Nichols said in Secrest's biography, "I already knew that Dalí was an abominable, heartless character. There was something supernaturally diabolical in Dalí ... and for years I have been unable to think of him without shuddering. Do you know, I was afraid of going blind!"

But if the painter had a reputation for being diabolical, his muse was not far behind. "Gala was an attractive, intelligent, ambitious, hard witch, without an atom of sensitivity of any kind. Hard and heartless," said Prince J.L. de Faucigny-Lucinge, Dalí's first real patron, who introduced the artist to the De Noailles in Paris, according to Secrest.

A critic of *The Secret Life* told the *New York Times* on 17 January 1943 that "Dalí frankly admits that he has made a fortune by exploiting people's stupidity," a stupidity concentrated mainly, in the USA, in the circles of fashion and the entertainment industry. In 1944 Dalí was commissioned to design the costumes and sets for a Spanish folklore show in Detroit; for the operetta *Mad Tristan*, based on a work by Wagner, in New York; and for the ballet *Sentimental Colloquy*.

In 1945, the Bignou Gallery opened an exhibition of paintings Dalí had produced in the US, and with the assistance of his old friend Met Miravitlles, they published a publicity newsletter entitled the *Dalí News*, imitating the heading and typeface of the *Daily News*.

That same year, just before the end of the Second World War, Alfred Hitchcock hired Dalí to paint sets for a number of scenes of the film *Spellbound*. Dalí duly did so, but some of the elements were so macabre they were cut by the American censors.

Dalí also illustrated de luxe book editions, including one of Shakespeare's *Macbeth*. He drew and painted advertisements for the fashion magazine *Vogue* and for various

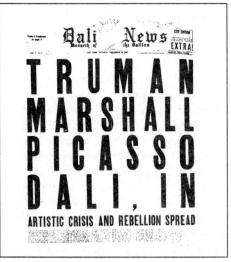

Dalí News, a Dalinian newsletter imitating the *Daily News*, created by Dalí and Miravitlles, November 1947. (GdC)

Essays of
MICHEL DE
Montaigne

TRANSLATED BY Charles Cotton
SELECTED AND ILLUSTRATED BY
Salvador Dali

DOUBLEDAY & COMPANY, INC.
Garden City, New York, 1947

One of the illustrations for the book *Essays of Michel de Montaigne*, New York, 1947. (GdC)

brands of perfumes and stockings, including Shocking, Bryan and Nylon, the latter appearing in the intellectual snobs' magazine the *New Yorker*.

Designing jewellery proved to be another continual and very lucrative sideline, not only for the Dalís but also for the legion of people who took part in it, from the unknown craftspeople who really made the pieces from Dalí's often hastily-sketched designs, to the manufacturers who mass-produced them, by way of all of the agents, representatives and finally the sellers. The business, based on the 'Dalí brand', still continues to flourish today, and is visible in display windows in airports throughout the capitalist world.

André Breton, by now a bitter adversary of Dalí, had played around with the letters of his enemy's name and come up with the anagram "Avida Dollars", which, apart from the obvious insult of referring directly to the artist's eagerness for riches (and using the feminine gender!), is also subtly reminiscent of the Latin names zoologists give to certain birds of prey.

The malicious nickname caught on quickly and was frequently quoted in writings about Dalí. But it would be unjust to attribute this material greed to Dalí alone. It was his muse, Gala, who counted the dollars and cents, not Dalí himself, who was always confused with currency exchanges and never had a clear idea of financial engineering. In any case, was he the only money-minded artist of his time? Did he not share this avidity for dollars with, for instance, the adult Picasso? The British writer James Lord, whose portrait Picasso painted, has said recently of latter (whom he calls "Stalin's arse-licker"), "Money is love, money is fame, and Picasso loved both of them all his life."

Despite his lasting commercial success in the United States, Dalí suffered the prodigal son syndrome. He wanted to walk on his beach in Cadaqués again, but visiting Spain was not advisable in the immediate aftermath of the World War. In 1946, the United Nations' General Assembly had condemned Franco's totalitarian regime and agreed on the recall of all ambassadors from Madrid. The situation in the Iberian Peninsula was unstable. There was still a possibility that the Allies might force the situation and topple the dictatorship, with Soviet influence then installing a communist regime.

But with the start of the Cold War, in 1947, the situation did an about-face. In the international geopolitical picture, Franco's anti-communist stance suddenly made Spain a priceless strategic bastion for defending the West from the Soviet menace, and soon there was talk of the Western allies lifting the sanctions on the dictatorship. Dalí, living as he was in the US, was better informed of the international situation than his compatriots in the Peninsula, who were subjected to strict censorship of radio and the press. He realised that a suitable moment had arrived, and in the summer of 1948 he returned to Spain. Two years later, the Western governments' ambassadors did the same.

At the same time, it is possible that, after living in the States for eight years, Dalí had reached the same cynical conclusion as William Waldorf Astor (a descendant of the English immigrant John Jacob Astor, who amassed a huge fortune in the fur trade in the first half of the 19th century and became the wealthiest man in the US): "The United States is all right for anyone who has to look for a way of making a living, but it isn't easy to understand why people who have travelled a lot and have enough money would stay there more than a week."

Picasso, 1947

CHAPTER 12

Home, sweet home

Cadaqués, 1948-50

In relating the famous parable of the prodigal son, the Gospel according to St Luke says, "But when he was yet a great way off, his father saw him, and had compassion, and ran, and fell on his neck, and kissed him." On 14 August 1948, the cover of the Barcelona magazine *Destino* proclaimed "Welcome to Salvador Dalí," and included a large photograph of the artist with his father. Old Mr. Dalí looks dejected, beaten, his eyes glazed, his face clamped in a rictus of concentrated anguish, while his son sits up as stiff as a statue, head high, eyes and nostrils flaring, staring defiantly into the photographer's lens.

The magazine's intention had been to enact the moment of reconciliation between father and son, which obviously would have been a story of human interest if it had really occurred. But the photograph itself insinuates the profound chasm that separated the two and the atmosphere of Greek tragedy that impregnated the house of the notary Mr. Dalí in Cadaqués. The article by *Destino's* reporter, Ignasi Agustí, was very long and highly praising of the artist. "We have spent three unforgettable days in Cadaqués," he wrote. But at no time did he mention that Salvador had been reunited with his sister. There are indications that she accompanied her father and, out of obligation, greeted and kissed her brother on his arrival in Cadaqués, but she undoubtedly kept her feelings, her bitterness, hidden.

The Dalís, father and son. Cover photo of the Barcelona magazine *Destino*, 14 August 1948. (ANC)

When he had been expelled from the paternal home before the Civil War, the young Dalí, recently coupled with Gala, had taken refuge in a row of old fishermen's huts in Portlligat, a small cove just outside Cadaqués. He gradually turned the huts into a cabin, and on his return from the US it rapidly became a splendid house by the water's edge, surrounded by olive trees, with a view dominated by the hill crowned by the old, baroque chapel of St Baldiri and a cemetery decorated with elegant funeral statues.

Gala, who one of the Surrealists had nicknamed "the whore of the steppes," would probably have been able to get on with life anywhere in the world. But Dalí had to 'go back home' to feel safe. It would not be exactly his father's

View of Portlligat in the 1980's. (GdC)

house, but it would be close by, and he would be able to sigh "Home, sweet home!" – if it were not for the fact that the domestic atmosphere of the Dalís' home resembled, more than anything, that of one of Hitchcock's sinister old houses.

Outwardly, Dalí had decided to stage another of his bizarre farces. Now he planned to pass himself off as a sincere convert to Catholicism, and – imitating the model of the perfect Christian family, a model very much in vogue in post-war Spain – in this comedy he would play the role of the God-fearing head of the household and Gala would be the devoted wife, and even his model for portraying the Mother of God!

On 23 November 1949, His Holiness Pope Pius XII received the couple in the Vatican. Dalí showed him an ink drawing entitled *The Madonna of Portlligat*, a carefully-prepared study for a large painting. The perfect features of the fictitious Madonna of Portlligat were those of a rejuvenated, idealised Gala.

As the Dalís emerged from the Papal audience, the Rome correspondent of the French magazine Carrefour recorded these declarations by the artist: "The world is suffering a crisis of materialism. Surrealism must incorporate itself into the evangelical order and continue the great tradition of religious art of the Middle Ages and the Renaissance. Modern art must be Christian!"

But Dalí could not fool many people, least of all his father and his sister. Old Mr. Dalí had known for years the true, painful explanation of his son's wild behaviour. "My son," he once confessed to his friend Josep Pla, "is abnormal." It was with this continuous, soul-searing observation that the artist's father had survived the last two decades. Now, old and worn, ill with cancer, with his son's wound deep in his heart, the retired notary Mr. Dalí was lying in his death bed. He passed away on 27 September 1950 and was buried in the discreet, isolated cemetery on the hill of St Baldiri, close to the chapel.

Salvador Dalí was not present at his father's burial nor his funeral mass, but the place he had chosen to be his home for the rest of his life lay in the shelter of the same hill. In the end, the wayward son had returned to the shadow of his father.

Fragment of the preparatory drawing of Gala as the model for *The Madonna of Portlligat*, 1950.

109

CHAPTER 13

The skin of the snake

Portlligat – New York – Portlligat, 1950's

The black telephone in Mr. Miravitlles' small, dark apartment in the city of skyscrapers rang insistently. Jaume 'Met' Miravitlles, Salvador Dalí's childhood friend, his collaborator in the scandalous films *Un chien andalou* and *L'âge d'or*, the ex-secretary of the Committee of Anti-Fascist Militias and ex-commissar of propaganda of the Government of Catalonia during the Civil War, was now living in exile in the USA, where he had become the New York correspondent of a news agency. He had to write an article a day to be distributed to twenty newspapers in Latin America. Consequently, he had to be alert to all opportunities, and the voice now speaking to him from the other end of the phone line always had something novel for him: it was the sonorous voice of Dalí. The artist was informing him that he was in New York again, but only for a short time, and that he would be waiting for him at the Hotel Saint Regis.

Not long after settling definitively in Portlligat, Dalí had realised that he could not stay still for long. Weak of character despite appearances, in business matters in particular Dalí allowed himself to be led along like a mule by Gala. And the evidence showed that the tandem Gala-Dalí had to continue to cultivate personally the dealings with their clients in Paris, still then the European capital of culture, and that they could not neglect the vital sounding-board that was New York. Without periodical reports from

New York via the international grapevine, the flame of Dalí's glory would gradually have sunk and died like a fire of kindling.

Moreover, Gala demanded that all purchases be paid in cash. No cheques, no bank transfers, no leads that could be followed by the taxman. Only dollars, francs, any hard currency, but on the barrelhead. That meant that they had to travel, and so the couple – or rather Gala – had decided to spend a short time each year in the US, another in Paris, and then return to their den in Portlligat.

Miravitlles described that 1958 meeting in New York with his old comrade as follows: "Dalí had told he was not feeling too well and that he would spend the afternoon in bed. At first we talked about Gaudí. Ever since he was little, and I can swear to this, Dalí has been a fanatic of Gaudí. Dalí believes in the magic of names, and the surnames Dalí and Gaudí sound exactly like the Catalan verbs *delir* and *gaudir*, which both mean to desire, to enjoy to the point of ecstasy…"

The interest inspired in Dalí's mind by the great Catalan architect Antoni Gaudí, the author of the extraordinary Temple of the Hoy Family in Barcelona, was similar to the admiration he felt for other extravagant Catalan figures, like Francesc Pujols. Pujols was a humorist, a dilettante, a self-taught philosopher, and his prose is a monument to the absurd, but some of his sayings are ingenious. Dalí had taken one of Pujol's books to New York with him, and according to Miravitlles, the scene proceeded as follows:

"Sitting up on the bed, wearing a pyjama jacket but no trousers, Dalí, who has always reminded me physically of Don Quixote, read me an absolutely crazy text by Francesc Pujols in which he established a comparison between the Catalan *escudella* [hotpot] and his philosophical and religious thought … At one moment, Dalí made an expression of acute pain, let out a terrible scream and fell down writhing on the bed. Alarmed, Gala called for the hotel doctor urgently. It was a brutal attack of appendicitis. An ambulance took him to the French Hospital in 30th Street. Gala and I went with him, and before going into the operating room he confessed to a chaplain and admitted that he was not married to Gala by the Church. The chaplain gave him the blessing on condition that he marry through the Catholic Church. Dalí promised that he would."

Miravitlles, who still occasionally assisted Dalí in his propaganda activities, refrained then from giving the press the unhappy news that the artist had been at the gates of death, that he had been saved, and that, for fear of dying, he had declared himself repentant before a priest. Precisely Dalí, who repeatedly said in public that did not repent of anything!

We are in no position to penetrate into the most intimate thoughts of Gala and Dalí. But seen from the outside, the continuation of the story is revealing: the couple decided to marry. The ceremony was held a few months later at the Gothic chapel of the Mare de Déu dels Àngels (Our Lady of the Angels), situated in a relatively isolated spot in the hills just east of Girona, more than fifty kilometres from their home in Cadaqués, a place reached only by a

Dalí with Met Miravitlles. (EG)

112

Girl of the Empordà, 1926

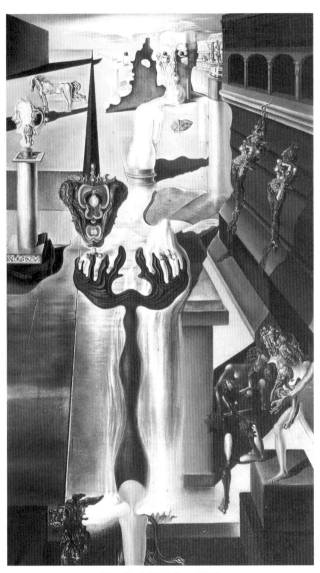

The Invisible Man, 1929

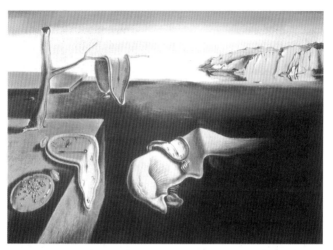

The persistance of Memory, 1931

Sleep, 1937

III

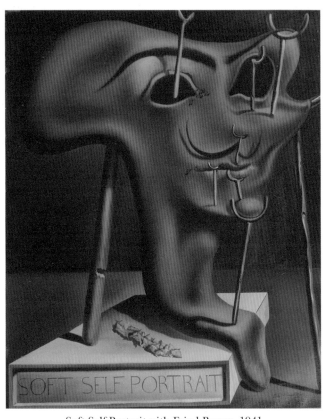

SOFT SELF PORTRAIT

Soft Self-Portrait with Fried Bacon, 1941

Galatea of the Spheres, 1952

Tristan and Isolda, 1944

The Three Enigmas of Gala, 1982

Explosion of Mystic Faith in the Centre of a Cathedral, 1974

Gala looking at the sea, which, at a distance of 18 metres,
becomes the portrait of Abraham Lincoln
(Homage of Rothko, 1976)

VIII

bumpy cart track. There was no photographer present at the ceremony.

When writing his memoirs in 1977 and 1978, Miravitlles, who was well informed of the artist's innermost thoughts, added, "Now Dalí is thinking of marrying through the Russian Coptic Church, which is his wife's. In this way, Dalí will be married twice to the same woman, who is the only one he has ever known, in the Biblical sense of the term."

Now that Dalí had come back to live in Catalonia after the long and intense eight years in the US, the Spanish press published a series of articles that spoke in his favour, but the journalist Manuel Brunet, a close friend Dalí's father and sister, sounded a note of alarm: "In these recent times, with no sense of responsibility whatsoever," he wrote in *Destino* in December 1949, "clouds of incense have been dedicated to Dalí, forgetting that he is the foremost pornographic painter of our time, the painter of the picture entitled *The Profanation of the Host* and the author of the book *Secret Life* ...Who was served by literary and pictorial Surrealism, with its anti-patriotic *bragadoccio* in all countries, with its blasphemous obscenities and extravagances? Is the vision of the fools so clouded? Do they not realise that, if this ideology, defended with insults and all manner of violence, reflected the true thought of Europe, we would all be heading for catastrophe?"

Dalí then found an obedient propagandist in the person of the journalist Josep Maria Massip, the New York correspondent of *Destino*. In reply to Massip's questions, and in prose evidently 'arranged' by the journalist himself, Dalí said, among other things, "At the current stage of my evolution I have the ambition of overcoming everything materialistic and atheistic there may be in Surrealism and incorporating its sources of inspiration into Spanish mysticism ... I was an atheist because of the experience of my childhood and adolescence; I am a mystic because of the experience of my youth."

Shortly before this, Anna Maria Dalí's book *Salvador Dalí seen by his Sister* had been published, narrating the other side of the family drama. Indignant, Dalí tirelessly sent cards and telegrams to the journalists to persuade them not to comment on Anna Maria's book. But in his interview with Massip he felt it appropriate to make, for the gallery, a conciliatory gesture towards his now terminally ill father, but without making any mention of his sister. "For me my father was, and continues to be, an exceptional personality," Dalí said. "I felt an enormous admiration for him. His words, his ideas and his gestures had a great influence on me, and I say that without any kind of resentment..."

Six months later his father died, and as we have seen, Dalí attended neither the burial nor the funeral mass.

It is true that Salvador Dalí had evolved. In his book *The Secret Life* he had already announced his need to change, like a snake shedding its skin. And from 1949 through the 1950's and into the early 60's, the most spectacular themes of Dalí's production were religious, in a version that aspired to be Catholic, apostolic and Roman.

Cover of *Manifeste Mystique*, a text with drawings by Dalí, published in Paris in 1951. (RJG)

After the small preparatory drawing he had made of *The Madonna of Portlligat*, Dalí painted a first version of the full-size picture in 1949. Imitating the composition of the Renaissance painters, the elements are arranged in parallel perspective, in which the vanishing point is centred and in infinity. The elements – a woman, a baby, a kind of chapel enclosing them – float in the air as separate pieces. Gala's face is drawn and painted with the perfection of an expert craftsman, as is the figure of the baby who is playing with a cross and a globe. In contrast, the mother's arms and hands are disproportionate, incorrect, as if they were painted by a different and less skilful hand.

But from the pictorial point of view, the great change is that here Dalí abandons the chaotic arrangement of his previous Surrealist paintings and returns to classical composition, and this was to be the style of his large canvases of the 1950's: a second large version of *The Madonna of Portlligat* (with arms and hands now correctly finished), purchased by the Minami group of companies of Tokyo; *Christ of St John of the Cross* (1951), bought by the Glasgow Art Gallery; *Crucifixion (Corpus Hypercubus)* (1954), bought by the New York Museum of Modern Art; *The Last Supper* (1955), bought by Chester Dale and donated to the National Gallery, Washington; *St James the Elder*, purchased by the Lord Beaverbrook Art Gallery of Frederickton, Nova Scotia, Canada; and *The Ecumenical Council*, now in the Salvador Dalí Museum in Saint Petersburg, Florida.

The snake of Dalí's art had clearly shed its old skin, but the reptile aroused a response in those who sensed its poison in their veins. Meryle Secrest says, "When the Glasgow Art Gallery bought the *Christ of St John of the Cross*, the reaction was totally hostile, and indeed the canvas was slashed by one furious visitor shortly after the opening of the exhibition."

When Paul J. Tillich, the famous German-born professor of theology and philosophy at Harvard University, was asked what he thought of *The Last Supper*, he indignantly

Presentation in Washington of the painting *The Last Supper*, 1955. (EG)

replied that it did not seem to him to be a religious painting, and that the Jesus Christ it portrayed looked "more like an American baseball player."

Even more outspoken was the writer John Canaday: "I suppose no-one is entitled to say of someone else that their religious conversion is an opportunistic attitude," he wrote. "But they are certainly entitled to say what they think of Dalí's indiscreet and annoying religious canvases, such as the *Last Supper* in the National Gallery in Washington ... It seems to me that they are the noisy expression of a morbid eroticism, where the artist has abused the right of asylum to the point of sacrilege."

CHAPTER 14

The man of the new times

Dalí's house in Portlligat stood a few paces from the sea, at the back of a rugged little bay encircled by hills which neither the ancient Phoenicians, Greeks nor Romans had dared or cared to explore during their stays in this region. In later times it became a refuge for poor fishermen, and was not discovered by the urbanites of contemporary society until the end of the 19th century. But the bare earth, the gnarled promontories, the arid coast with its lobsters, sea urchins and rock mussels as its most illustrious inhabitants, and a light as marvellous as that of Provence, finally drew the attention of a number of Impressionist artists, like the Barcelona landscape painter Eliseu Meifrèn, who discovered there the force of virgin nature.

I went to interview Dalí in Portlligat in the summer of 1965, accompanied by the photographer Anna Baldazzi of the magazine *Le Ore*, at that time the Italian counterpart of France's *Paris-Match* or Germany's *Stern*.

Seen from the outside, the artist's house, all whitewashed, was not dissimilar to the two or three others that had been built close to it. The knotty olive trees and lofty cypresses that surrounded the house were an invitation to peace. But on going through the narrow entrance gate, you had the impression of stepping into the backstage area of a circus.

In the entrance stood a desiccated bear wearing a necklace. Further inside, one corner was adorned by a colossal

117

elephant's tusk. A suit-and-tied assistant asked us, with a few words, to wait on the terrace, where, half hidden under a prickly cactus, a stereo unit sent the delicately-poised notes of a piece by Bach drifting through the air, accompanied by the monotonous scratching of the needle of the record player. Suddenly there was an apparition before us. We had not heard a single footstep, but there he was, standing stock still, and his motionless eyes fixed us like those of a black cat you suddenly come across with a shock amid some old ruins. It was Dalí's stare.

His dark shirt with its white trimmings and large white floral design made him look like something between a lion tamer and a rock'n'roll singer. But on closer inspection, the two large flowers on the chest turned out to be *fleur-de-lys*, the heraldic symbol of the royal house of France.

When I told him of my genuine interest in knowing something about his painting techniques, Dalí showed me into his *sancta sanctorum*. In one corner there hung a framed photograph of about 24 by 30 centimetres of José Antonio Primo de Rivera, the founder of the Falange, the Spanish Fascist party. It was a copy of the typical matt photo that had hung in virtually all official buildings and

Dalí with Joan Castellar-Gassol, Portlligat, 1965. (AB)

schools in Spain since the end of the Civil War. In another corner hung another photo, of the same size, the same matt tone, in an identical frame: and the character appearing in it was none other than Josif Stalin.

Apart from these details, so foreign to art, the rest of the studio looked much like any other painter's den. The age-old rush-bottomed chair of the typical Catalan rural home was there, in front of the easel, beside the little table with paint pots holding the long brushes. Dalí liked to be portrayed with his right hand outstretched, holding a long-handled paintbrush, and examining the picture from a distance, in deliberate imitation of the clichéd attitude of painters caricatured in cartoons. In fact, Dalí used short, fine brushes to achieve the obsessive, minute detail of his work.

In his large compositions he often copied from enlarged photographs, on which he drew a grid in pencil in order to work on each of the parts in detail, as did the painters of the Renaissance and the Enlightenment. His painting *Christ of St John of the Cross*, which has been endlessly reproduced in postcards, is a spectacular feat of optical illusionism. But whether the end result was more harmonic or less so, or even not at all, the profound sensation you had was that everything was artificial, frozen, unhealthy, disassociated from nature and life – nothing to do with the *joie de vivre* with which Eliseu Meifrèn had painted Cadaqués in 1886.

Conversation with Dalí, if it did not go on too long, could be truly stimulating – especially, perhaps, for someone talking to him for the first and last time. He was gifted with a greater than average natural intelligence, but his mental agility was constantly impeded by the incessant bombardment of dispersed ideas that could shoot through his brain like a meteorite shower at any moment.

From his reading of books and the press, he captured with rapid perspicacity what journalists called 'current issues' – at a time when 'current' could be something that lasted for weeks or months, not mere days or minutes like now. He sensed that certain topics would be material for slow reflection on the part of intellectuals, scientists and politicians and would be 'fashionable' in the coming years. He possessed the innate gift of foresight, of seeing things approaching over the horizon, which he applied with imperturbable patience to his task of perpetual self-promotion. A task in which, incidentally, various teams of people also worked, not always visibly, under the strict inspection or remote control of Gala.

Dalí could combine a quotation from Einstein that he had learned in the United States with a piece of nonsense typical of a café argument in Figueres, and he would amuse himself with very earthy Catalan wordplay, mixing in the odd French expression. But this sparkling and relatively 'normal' talk would soon come to an end: suddenly, unleashed, he would launch pompously into a solemn monologue, as if making a speech to the stuffy members of the Académie Française.

In those days, as an integral part of the Cold War, the superpowers were beginning to explore space, and it was expected that an attempt would soon be made to send men to the moon. The images of astronauts floating weightlessly in space had captured the whole world's attention. And Dalí had already used this imagery back in 1950, in his painting *The Madonna of Portlligat*, where the Madonna herself and all the other elements of the picture seem to be weightless bodies. "Weightlessness is the symbol of our time," Dalí said, waiting for me to take good note of his words. "That is what Le Corbusier never understood. Precisely on the day Le Corbusier died, I, Dalí, was giving a speech about weightlessness. Le Corbusier is a symbol of everything that is solid, static: it's out of date. I am the man of the new times."

Then he amused himself by clothing a dummy in a dress he had invented, on which he had painted a space rocket, and once dressed, he violently tore its stomach open to produce a sado-masochistic effect. It was the inevitable perverse detail revealing that the show, duly photographed, had truly been a product of the 'Dalí factory.'

In fact, the 'factory' was on the way to becoming a powerful multinational corporation. It was Dalí's own sister, Anna Maria, who had said, "Since 1949, Dalí has been promoted as a character that he has found himself forced to play ... For those who manufactured the *Dalí character*, the economic success has been absolute, it could not be more profitable for them."

And naturally one single worker could not do everything. The woodcuts of the series *The Divine Comedy* bearing Dalí's signature, published by J. Foret in Paris in 1960, certainly seemed to have been created by the hands of our man, but some of the drawings that illustrated the book *Casanova*, published in Paris in 1967 by the Cercle du Livre Précieux, could have been done by a cynical amateur erotomaniac. The suspicion was in the air: if there were dozens of forgeries of Picassos, why should there not also be fakes of "the man of the new times" of Portlligat?

CHAPTER 15

And the world will admire me

The autumn of 1987 seemed to be a good moment for the opening in Japan of an exhibition of three hundred engravings and lithographs signed by Dalí. It was planned that the exhibition, organised by the *Kobe Shimbun* newspaper in the city of Kobe and sponsored by the Government of Catalonia, would then be presented in other Japanese cities. At the *vernissage*, the guests' Oriental smiles, however inscrutable, augured success. Just one small problem reared its head: some of the items on show were probably forgeries.

The French dealer Robert Descharnes, who was then Dalí's representative and also the proprietor of the Dutch art firm Demart, threatened to report the *Kobe Shimbun* to the police for exhibiting works whose authenticity was "in doubt". At that time Descharnes was at daggers drawn with the Catalan agent Enric Sabater, who had represented Dalí between 1974 and 1980.

Under the heading 'Descharnes and Sabater fight over the royalties,' the Spanish news agency Efe reported: 'Josep Miquel García, the coordinator of the plastic arts service of the Government of Catalonia, said that "the claims being made by Descharnes' firm Demart are unfounded." However, the Kobe Museum has decided to withdraw 30 works, and the exhibition planned for the city of Sapporo has been cancelled.' In turn, Sabater, siding with García, accused Descharnes of "disseminating fake Dalís in the international market."

It had been public knowledge for years that many of the paintings, lithographs, engravings and other works attributed to Dalí were really imitations, and that they represented millions of dollars' worth of sales.

There were witnesses. For a time, the Catalan skipper David Guasch captained the British yacht *Ilex* which belonged to the Englishman John Peter Moore, who had worked for Dalí until 1974 and was known around Cadaqués as 'Captain Moore'. Guasch has said, "During two summers while I was in Cadaqués, a British-registered yacht called *Rampage* anchored there. It was an impressive boat. As soon as it arrived, its launch headed for the shore, to Dalí's house, carrying two enormous packages of blank sheets of paper. Then they placed the sheets on a table. Dalí sat in the middle, with an assistant on either side, and started signing the blank sheets one after the other. And of course, if at the same time, or later, they sent a plate with the original engraved drawing, they could make as many copies as they liked with any system of reproduction. Traditionally, a very limited edition is made from each original, but in this case they ignored the rules. For each Dalí signature print they could make 800 dollars in the USA. But I've always believed that some of the people who were around Dalí in the 70's and 80's made more money than he did."

Apart from the uncontrolled editions of lithographs signed by Dalí himself, there was another, shadier and perhaps more lucrative activity: selling items that were falsely passed off as Dalí's work, bearing his forged signature. One of the artists who worked in these operations is Manuel Pujol Baladas, a Catalan painter born in 1947 who in his own works has demonstrated an extraordinary mastery of both the pencil and the brush. Pujol was once an auxiliary teacher of the Massana Art School in Barcelona, and later the artistic director of a publicity firm. At a certain moment he came into contact with the Dalí clan, and this is his story:

The painter Manuel Pujol Baladas imitates Dalí's signature in front of Joan Castellar-Gassol in his Barcelona workshop, 1987. (GUMI)

"Gala knew that I was a painter, and she asked me to show her some of my work, because she said I had a lot of talent. I did so, and she told me, 'You paint well, but you've got no commercial vision. If you take my advice you can be very successful.' At first I said I wasn't interested, but later, about to be a father for the second time and seeing that my attempts to establish myself as an independent artist were not prospering, I fell into the trap. Some close friends of Enric Sabater, who was then Dalí and Gala's right-hand man, came to see me and proposed that I paint some *Dalís*, because Dalí couldn't control the trembling in his hands. I started painting and painting, and there were days when I would do as many as six pieces, making them up out of my head. It was creative work. My works were intended to be marketed as authentic Dalís, and the snowball just got bigger and bigger. 'My' Dalís began to appear in 1976 and 1977. They were mostly drawings, watercolours, gouaches and a few oils. In total, about 530 pieces. And I calculate that by 1981 my production of imitations on paper had exceeded Dalí's own in quantity."

According to Manuel Pujol, in the Dalí Museum in Cleveland, Ohio – which contained the Reynolds Morse collection later transferred to Saint Petersburg, Florida – there was one of 'his' Dalís. And a painting of an elephant displayed in the Museum of Bogotà, Colombia, and officially attributed to Dalí, is also his.

"What's more," says Pujol, "two works of mine displayed in the Tate Gallery in London and later auctioned at Sotheby's were believed to be by Dalí."

Manuel Pujol had a very hard time when he tried to get out of the business and rehabilitate his name, and was even threatened with reprisals reminiscent of 1920's Chicago.

After the death of Gala in 1982, with Dalí's spirit broken, the rivalries between the various dealers who had got rich on his work began to make themselves plain. One of the angriest was Pierre Argillet, from Paris, a publisher of pornographic books, eight of which had been illustrated by Dalí. Two of the most notable volumes were *Poèmes secrets* by Apollinaire, printed in 1967, and *La Venus des fourrures*, (*Venus in Furs*), by the 19th-century Austrian novelist Leopold von Sacher-Masoch (whose name and work inspired the term 'masochism'), for which Dalí produced sixteen appropriate engravings. But Argillet was not pleased with his competitors, particularly with Moore and Descharnes, and in September 1984, with Dalí seriously ill, he travelled to Catalonia with the intention of stirring things up. "I have come to Barcelona to find out about the state of health of my good friend Dalí," he told the press, "but I have also come to try to make the Spanish authorities stop the proliferation of false engravings." The Parisian publisher accused Moore of having supplied a stock of blank sheets signed by Dalí which had been used to produce 35,000 engravings, and accused Descharnes of being "too permissive" regarding the royalties.

As for the fortunes that were made by Dalí's collaborators or dealers, there are only indications, and unreliable ones at that. At the end of the 1980's it was written, and never denied, that Enric Sabater's fortune was calculated at nearly 2,000 million pesetas (some fifteen million dollars of the time). According to Meryle Secrest, in 1970, twenty years earlier, Dalí's own fortune was estimated at some ten million dollars.

In 1970, Dalí had bought a small, abandoned Gothic castle in the tiny Empordanese village of Púbol, some forty kilometres south-west of Cadaqués, and turned it into a residence exclusively for Gala, although he did live there for a while. By now the two were tired of each other: Dalí's psychopathological dependence on Gala still persisted, but she had squeezed out of him all she wanted and no longer needed him.

At the age of approximately 74 (her exact year of birth has never been established), Hélène Ivánovna Diákonova, alias Gala, alias the praying mantis, alias the whore of the steppes, was suffering from an acute case of nympho-mania, and the favours she needed to buy from a varied succession of young men required a comfortable and discreet location. The village of Púbol, with a census of only 129 in-habitants, was certainly discreet, and the castle, standing beside the church at the highest point of the village, would be comfortable once it was restored. Outside it might look like a castle from the Middle Ages, but inside, Dalí's out-landish decoration gave it an air partly of Disneyland, partly of the Marquis de Sade's mansion, with the inevitable macabre detail: the basement was to house the crypt where the mistress of the castle was to be put to rest after her death. And indeed, it was in this Frankensteinian haunt that Gala's body was laid in June 1982. The shroud matched the setting, for it was the colour of blood, a rabidly bright red dress, according to Gala's wishes, it is said. A dress that bore the label 'Dior'.

In December 1980, realising that her time was running out, Gala made her will and took the opportunity to show the world, for one last time, what kind of heart she had. The will explicitly said that she left nothing to Cécile, her daughter by her first husband, Paul Grindel, alias Paul Éluard.

An aversion to the family had been one of the longest-lasting feelings Gala and Dalí had shared, and Dalí chan-nelled this aversion towards the famous painting *L'Angélus* by Jean-François Millet, conserved in the Louvre in Paris, in which the Norman painter immortalised a couple of young farm workers. From their bowed posture and earth-ward gaze, the viewer deduces that they are giving thanks to God for the day's provisions, however meagre, on hearing the vespers bell, and the picture evokes the harmony of the human family united in both misfortune and hope.

Millet's painting was very popular; it had been repro-duced many times in both France and Catalonia, and had even illustrated a calendar that was hung in countless homes and schools. Dalí had seen it in his school, and ever since then he had poured scorn on it. He imagined, against all the evidence, that the woman's submissive attitude, with her back bent slightly forwards, suggested only one thing: her desire to be penetrated anally by her husband. On this demented assumption, Dalí painted three transformations of Millet's picture in the 1930's, and even in 1965 he amused himself with coloured pencils to make an explicitly pornographic drawing which, adding insult to injury, he entitled *Homage to Millet*.

This drawing forms part of Dalí's voluminous legacy to the Spanish State, by virtue of his last will and testament made in September 1982 in the castle of Púbol, where he had gone to live temporarily after Gala's death. (The will entirely excluded his sister Anna Maria.) In gratitude for services rendered to the State, the King of Spain created an *ad hoc* noble title for the artist: 'Marquis of Dalí and Púbol.'

If, one stormy night, a bolt of lightning had struck the ghostly castle and burned it down, people could have said that the cause had been the wrath of the gods. But the official version was that it was simply a spark from a short-circuit that had caused a fire in Dalí's bedroom in the early hours of 30 August 1984.

More dead than alive, Dalí had to be rescued, with some difficulty, from the blazing room. The fire brigade, arriving at dawn, managed to prevent the fire from devouring the rest of the smoke-shrouded castle.

Dalí was transferred to Figueres, where he lived on for a further four years and five months. His last home, the scene of his artificially-prolonged agony, was the building originally known as the Torre Gorgot but renamed Torre Galatea at Dalí's wish, a mansion standing next to the town's Municipal Theatre, which in 1974 had been converted into the Dalí Theatre-Museum.

In keeping with the precedent of the tomb site chosen by Gala, and, going back thousands of years, the places where the Pharaohs had had themselves buried, the man

128

who as an adolescent had written "I will be a genius and the world will admire me" wanted to be interred in a funeral chamber in his own monumental building.

His last wish was respected. When he died, on 23 January 1989, his remains were clothed in a light-coloured tunic with a heraldic coronet embroidered on it, and laid in a tomb set into what was formerly the stage of the theatre. The inscription on the stone is as laconic and cold as the marble itself:

Salvador Dalí i Domènech
Marquis of Dalí and Púbol
1904-1989

CHRONOLOGY

1904 11 May: birth of Salvador Dalí in the town of Figueres (Empordà, Catalonia).

1907 In Paris, Picasso paints what is considered the first Cubist picture.

1908 Anna Maria Dalí, the artist's sister, is born in Figueres.

1909 22 February: the Parisian newspaper *Le Figaro* publishes *Futurism*, a manifesto by the Italian intellectual F.T. Marinetti.

1910 Salvador Dalí enters the Hispano-French School in Figueres.

1914 Beginning of the First World War.

1915 The painter Giorgio di Chirico, resident in Paris, exhibits his *Metaphysical Painting*, a precursor of Surrealism.

1916 Dalí begins his secondary education and drawing studies at the Municipal School of Figueres.
      In Zürich, Tristan Tzara publishes the *Dada Manifesto.*

1917 The October Revolution in Russia brings the Bolsheviks to power.

1918 End of the First World War.

1919 Dalí participates in collective exhibitions in his home town.

1920 In Paris, the Catalan painter Joan Miró comes into contact with the Surrealists.

1921 Dalí's mother, Felipa Domènech, dies at the age of 47. His father marries Caterina, Felipa's sister.

1922 After exhibiting in Barcelona, Dalí enters the Academy of San Fernando art school in Madrid, living at the city's Students' Residence, where he meets Federico García Lorca and Luis Buñuel.

1923	Dalí is expelled from the Academy of San Fernando.
1924	Dalí is imprisoned by the police of the new dictatorial regime.
	In Paris, André Breton publishes the *Surrealist Manifesto*.
	In Rome, Marinetti publishes *Futurism and Fascism*.
1925	Dalí spends his holidays in Cadaqués, on the Costa Brava near Figueres, in the company of Lorca.
	In Paris, the first collective exhibition by the Surrealists.
1926	Dalí travels to Paris for the first time, to meet Picasso.
	June: death of the Catalan architect Antoni Gaudí.
	Autumn: Dalí exhibits in Barcelona, beside canvases by Dufy, Miró and others.
1927	Dalí begins his compulsory military service in Figueres.
1928	F.T. Marinetti declares that Dalí is one of his followers.
1929	Dalí meets Gala, the wife of the French poet Paul Éluard.
	Premiere in Paris of the film *Un chien andalou* by Buñuel and Dalí.
	Dalí is expelled from his father's home for having insulted the memory of his mother.
	Wall Street Crash.
1930	Dalí scandalises the audience at the Ateneu Barcelonès by insulting the memory of the popular Catalan romantic dramatist Àngel Guimerà.
	In Paris, the magazine *Surrealism at the Service of the Revolution* appears.
	The Second International Revolutionary Writers' Congress, associated with the French Communist Party, attacks Surrealism.
1931	Young French patriots attack the Parisian cinema where Buñuel and Dalí's second film, *L'âge d'or*, has just been premiered.
	The Catalan journalist Jaume ('Met') Miravitlles, a friend of Dalí's, publishes *Against Bourgeois Culture*, in which he relates Surrealism with Marxism.
	In Spain, the Republic is proclaimed.
1932	Works by Dalí are exhibited at the Julien Levy gallery in New York.
1934	Dalí and Gala spend four months in New York.
1936	The International Surrealist Exhibition opens in London.

Start of the Spanish Civil War. In Andalusia, Fascists assassinate García Lorca.

Time magazine dedicates its cover to Dalí.

1937   Aircraft of the German Condor Legion at the service of Franco bombard the Basque town of Gernika.

1938   Surrealist exhibition in Paris.

Nazi invasion of Austria.

The Condor Legion bombards Barcelona.

Dalí and Gala move into Coco Chanel's house near Monte Carlo.

1939   January: Barcelona is occupied by Franco's troops.

March: Dalí, living temporarily in New York, is arrested for breach of the peace after an incident at the Bonwit-Teller store.

April: end of the Spanish Civil War.

September: start of the Second World War.

1940   14 June: Nazi troops occupy Paris. Dalí and Gala flee to New York via Lisbon.

1941   The New York Museum of Modern Art exhibits works by Dalí.

Breton breaks off relationships with Dalí.

1942   *The Secret Life of Salvador Dalí by Salvador Dalí* is published in New York.

1943   Death of Marinetti.

Dalí paints advertising posters for brands of perfume, stockings and ties.

1945   Premiere in the USA of Alfred Hitchcock's film *Spellbound*, with sets by Dalí.

August: end of the Second World War.

1946   The UN condemns Franco's totalitarian regime and agrees to recall all foreign ambassadors from Madrid.

1948   Dalí and Gala return to Spain.

1949   Dalí and Gala are received by Pope Pius XII at the Vatican.

In Barcelona, Anna Maria Dalí's book *Salvador Dalí seen by his Sister* is published.

1950   Dalí gives a speech at the Ateneu Barcelonès entitled *Why was I sacrilegious, why am I mystical?*

Dalí's father dies of cancer.

1966   Death of André Breton.

1970	Dalí buys the Gothic castle in Púbol (Empordà) as Gala's private residence.
1971	A Salvador Dalí Museum is inaugurated in Cleveland, Ohio, with works belonging to Reynolds Morse. The collection is later transferred to Saint Petersburg, Florida.
1973	Death of Picasso.
1974	The Dalí Theatre-Museum is opened in Figueres.
1975	Death of Franco.
1982	Gala dies and is buried in the castle of Púbol.
1983	Death of Joan Miró.
	Death of Luis Buñuel.
1989	Death of Salvador Dalí. He is buried in the Dalí Theatre-Museum in Figueres.
1990	Anna Maria Dalí, the artist's sister, dies in Cadaqués at the age of 82.
2004	Centenary of the birth of Salvador Dalí.

BIBLIOGRAPHY

BEYA I MARTÍ, Pere: *Llers.* Gràfiques Canigó (Figueres, 1992).

BUÑUEL, Luis: *Mon dernier soupir.* R. Laffont (Paris, 1982).

CERVERA I BERTA, Mossèn Josep M.: *Un rector màrtir. Mossèn Pere Arolas i Vergés.* Gràfiques Montserrat, S.A. (Figueres, 1990).

CHAMBERLAIN, Lesley: *The Secret Artist: A Close Reading of Sigmund Freud.* Quartet (London, 2001).

CORTÈS I VIDAL, Joan: *Setanta anys de vida artística barcelonina.* Ed. Selecta (Barcelona, 1980).

DALÍ, Anna Maria: *Tot l'any a Cadaqués.* Ed. Joventut (Barcelona, 1982).

— *Salvador Dalí visto por su hermana.* (Translated from the Catalan by Maria Luz Morales.) Ed. Joventut (Barcelona, 1949).

— *Salvador Dalí visto por su hermana.* Prologue by Ian Gibson. Ed. Parsifal (Barcelona, 1993).

— *Noves imatges de Salvador Dalí.* Ed. Columna (with the support of the Municipal Council of Cadaqués). Prologue by Jaume Maurici (Barcelona, 1988).

DALÍ, Salvador: *The Secret Life of Salvador Dalí.* Dial Press (New York, 1942).

— *La vie secrète de Salvador Dalí.* Gallimard/La Table Ronde (Paris, 1952).

— *La vida secreta de Salvador Dalí.* Dasa Ediciones (Barcelona, 1981).

— *La conquête de l'irrationel.* Éditions Surréalistes (Paris, 1935).

DUCHAMP, Marcel: *Affect. Marcel. The Selected Correspondence of Marcel Duchamp.* F.M. Naumann and H. Obalk, editors. Thames and Hudson (London, 2001).

FAGES DE CLIMENT, C.: *Les bruixes de Llers.* Pòrtic de Ventura Gassol. Definitive version. Edited by Montserrat Vayreda and Jaume Maurici. Aubert Impressor (Olot, 1977).

FORNÉS, Eduard: *Les contradiccions del cas Dalí*. Llibres de l'Avui (Barcelona, 1989).

FREUD, Sigmund: *Le mot d'esprit et ses rapports avec l'inconscient*. Gallimard (Paris, 1953).

GENTILE, Giovanni: *Origini e dottrina del fascismo*. Libreria Littorio. Quaderni dell'Istituto Nazionale Fascista di Cultura (Rome, 1929).

GIBSON, Ian: *The Shameful Life of Salvador Dalí*. Faber and Faber (London, 1997).

GIMÉNEZ CABALLERO, Ernesto: *Genio de España*. Ed. Jerarquía. 3rd edition (Zaragoza, 1938).

— *Genio de España*. 7th edition, with '*Epílogo sobre hoy*'. Ed. Doncel (Madrid, 1971).

— *Julepe de Menta*. Cuadernos Literarios (Madrid, 1929).

GUARDIOLA I ROVIRA, Ramon: *Dalí a primera mà*. Editorial Gironina, S.A. (Girona, 1990).

HAUSER, Arnold: *The Social History of Art*. Routledge & Kegan Paul (London, 1951).

KOESTLER, Arthur: *The Act of Creation*. Penguin Books (London, 1989).

LEIRIS, Michel: *L'âge d'homme*. N.R.F. (Paris, 1939).

LLADÓ I FIGUERAS, Josep Maria: *Homenatge a vint-i-vuit catalans eminents*. Generalitat de Catalunya (Barcelona, 1992).

LOMAS, David: *The Haunted Self: Surrealism, Psychoanalysis, Subjectivity*. Yale University Press (Yale, 2001).

MIRAVITLLES, Jaume: *Contra la cultura burgesa*. L'Hora (Barcelona, no date, probably 1931).

NADEAU, Maurice: *Histoire du surréalisme*. Seuil (Paris, 1948).

— *Historia del surrealismo*. Prologue by Raúl Navarro. S. Rueda, editor (Buenos Aires, 1948).

NÉRET, Gilles: *Dalí*. Taschen (Cologne, 2000).

OLIVAR, M.: *Cien obras maestras de la pintura*. Ed. Salvat (Barcelona, 1969).

ORWELL, George: *Homage to Catalonia*. Harcourt Brace (New York, 1952).

PETOCZ, Agnes: *Freud, Psychoanalysis and Symbolism*. Cambridge University Press (Cambridge, 2001).

PLA, Josep: *Retrats de passaport*. Ed. Destino (Barcelona, 1991).

READ, Peter: *Apollinaire et 'Les mamelles de Tirésias'*. Presses Universitaires de Rennes (Rennes, 2001).

Romero, Luis: *Dedalico Dalí.* Ed. B (Barcelona, 1989).

Santos Torroella, Rafael: *La trágica vida de Salvador Dalí.* Ed. Parsifal (Barcelona, 1995).

Schneider, Herbert: *Making the Fascist State.* Oxford University Press (New York, 1920).

Secrest, Meryle: *Salvador Dalí: the Extravagant Surrealist.* Epilogue by André Thirion. Hachette (Paris, 1988).

Tharrats, Joan Josep: *Cent anys de pintura a Cadaqués.* Ed. del Cotal (Barcelona, 1981).

ARTICLES AND ESSAYS

Agustí, Ignacio: *Bienvenida a Salvador Dalí.* Destino, nº 575 (Barcelona, 14 August 1948).

Bell, Clive: *The Zwemmer Gallery.* New Statesman and Nation (London, 22 December 1934).

Bellmunt, Domènec de: *El pintor de Cadaqués.* Avui (Barcelona, 3 September 1980).

Blunt, Anthony: *The Beaver and the Silkworm.* The Spectator (London, 2 November 1934).

Bou, Enric: *'Nightmare Journey': Dalí als Estats Units.* V Jornades d'Estudis Catalano-Americans. Generalitat de Catalunya (Barcelona, 1997).

Brownrigg, Sylvia: *Sinister Original.* The Times Literary Supplement (London, 6 June 2001).

Brunet, Manuel: *Salvador Dalí visto por su hermana.* Destino, nº 647 (Barcelona, 31 December 1949).

Cadilhac, Paul-Émile: *États-Unis 1937.* L'Illustration (Paris, 10 April 1937).

Caro Baroja, Julio: *Madrid.* Información Comercial Española, nº 402. Ministerio de Comercio (Madrid, 1967).

Casademont, Emili: *Darrer Acte. Crònica de Figueres.* Xarxa, nº 2 (Barcelona, November 1987).

Castellar-Gassol, J.: *Dalí: cómo prepara uno de sus gags.* Índice, nº 209 (Madrid, 1966).

— *Max Ernst en la tradición surrealista.* Temas de Arquitectura (Madrid, January 1968).

— *Hospital español del arte.* Selecciones del Reader's Digest (Madrid, April 1971).

— *Dalí i els altres Dalís*. Xarxa, nº 2 (Barcelona, November 1987).

— *Three craftsmen, one country. Rigau, Fortuny, Sert*. Made in Catalunya, nº 2 (Barcelona, May-June 1989).

— *El revival de Santiago Rusiñol*. Notícies de la Generalitat de Catalunya, nº 134 (Barcelona, November 1997).

CHEVENIER, Robert: *Comment fonctionne le controle de non-intervention*. L'Illustration, nº 4918 (Paris, 5 June 1937).

DEVREE, Howard: *Secret Life of Salvador Dalí*. The New York Times (New York, 18 January 1943).

FRANCHINI, Claude: *Les oiseaux Hitch et la catharsis*. Contre-champ, mensuel de critique cinématografique, nº 6-7 (Marseilles, 1963).

GREENBERG, Clement: *The Jackson Pollock market wars*. The New York Times Magazine (New York, 16 April 1961).

IONESCO, Eugène: *Précurseurs roumains de surréalisme*. Les Lettres Nouvelles (Paris, January-February 1965).

KENT, George: *Íntimo y simbólico Joan Miró*. Selecciones del Reader's Digest (Madrid, January 1971).

LORD, James: *Stalin's painter*. The Times Literary Supplement (London, 30 March 2001).

LUBAR, Robert S.: *Miró, Dalí and their American critics in 1941*. IV Jornades d'Estudis Catalano-Americans. Generalitat de Catalunya (Barcelona, 1992).

MASSIP, José M.: *Dalí, hoy*. Destino, nº 660 (Barcelona, 1 April 1950).

MIRAVITLLES, Jaume: *Salvador Dalí i Francesc Pujols*. In *Gent que he conegut*, Ed. Destino (Barcelona, 1980).

MOLAS, Joaquim: *Salvador Dalí: entre el surrealisme i el marxisme*. In *Dalí i els llibres*, Generalitat de Catalunya (Barcelona, 1982).

ORWELL, George: *Raffles and Mrs. Blandish*. Horizon. *The Collected Essays of George Orwell, volume 3*. Penguin Books (London, 1970).

PÉREZ, Javier: Nuevas figuraciones. Supplement nº 7, Arte (Madrid, 2001).

PLA, Josep: *Salvador Dalí, una notícia*. In *Josep Pla, Obra Completa, vol. 29*. Ed. Destino (Barcelona, 1991).

RAMOS, Rafael: *Londres inaugura un Museo Dalí*. La Vanguardia (Barcelona, 4 June 2000).

REGÀS, Rosa: *Salvador Dalí: "En las mujeres adoro el universo"*. Siglo 20 (Barcelona, 26 June 1965).

— *Show Dalí.* Siglo 20 (Barcelona, 11 September 1965).

SANCHIS, Imma: *Hoy los museos son puro marketing.* La Vanguardia (Barcelona, 5 April 2001).

SANTOS TORROELLA, Rafael: *Francis Picabia i Barcelona.* Catalogue-book of the anthological exhibition. Ministerio de Cultura – Fundació Caixa de Pensions (Barcelona, 1985).

SARGEANT, Winthrop: *Dalí: an excitable Spanish artist.* Life (New York, 24 September 1945).

SASOT, Mario: *Buñuel, pornógrafo frustrado.* La Vanguardia (Barcelona, 24 February 2001).

SEGARRA, Ignasi: *Animal Farm '50.* Diari de Tarragona (Tarragona, 11 September 1995).

SENTÍS, Carles: *Castillos en España y el fácil norteamericano.* Destino (Barcelona, 17 August 1940).

— *Secretos a voces.* Destino (Barcelona, 24 August 1940).

VAL, Eusebio: *Una exposición reconcilia Alemania con el futurismo afín a Mussolini.* La Vanguardia (Barcelona, 11 March 2001).

CATALOGUES, PAMPHLETS AND OTHER PUBLICATIONS

Dalí i els llibres. Exhibition catalogue. Generalitat de Catalunya (Barcelona, 1982).

Dalí: els anys joves. Exhibition catalogue. Departament de Cultura de la Generalitat de Catalunya (Barcelona, 1982).

Picabia. Catalogue-book of the anthological exhibition. Ministerio de Cultura – Fundació Caixa de Pensions (Barcelona, 1985).

Salvador Dalí: Programa d'activitats. Museu Abelló (Mollet del Vallès, 2001).

J. CASTELLAR-GASSOL has written for the Reader's Digest and has been Associate Writer of the magazine *Cambio 16* and director of the magazine CULTURA, published by the Government of Catalonia. He is an ex-student of Ruskin College, Oxford, and a member of the Association of Writers in the Catalan Language and the European Writers' Association.

KEY TO SOURCES OF ILLUSTRATIONS: